the pop classics series

extra salty

jennifer's body

frederick blichert

ecwpress

Published by ECW Press
665 Gerrard St. East
Toronto, Ontario, Canada M4M 1Y2
416-694-3348 / info@ecwpress.com

Editors for the press: Crissy Calhoun and
Jennifer Knoch
Cover and text design: David Gee

Library and Archives Canada Cataloguing in
Publication

Title: Extra salty : Jennifer's body / Frederick
Blichert.

Other titles: Jennifer's body

Names: Blichert, Frederick, author.

Series: Pop classic series ; #11.

Description: Series statement: The pop classics
series ; #11

Identifiers: Canadiana (print) 20210209909 |
Canadiana (ebook) 20210210443

ISBN 978-1-77041-589-8 (softcover)
ISBN 978-1-77305-803-0 (ePub)
ISBN 978-1-77305-804-7 (PDF)
ISBN 978-1-77305-805-4 (Kindle)

Subjects: LCSH: Jennifer's body (Motion
picture) | LCSH: Sex role in motion pictures.
| LCSH: Women in motion pictures. | LCSH:
Feminism and motion pictures.

Classification: LCC PN1997.2.J46 B55 2021
| DDC 791.43/72—dc23

Printing: Friesens   5   4   3   2   1
PRINTED AND BOUND IN CANADA

This book is funded in part by the Government of Canada. *Ce livre est financé en partie par
le gouvernement du Canada.* We also acknowledge the support of the Government of Ontario
through the Ontario Book Publishing Tax Credit, and through Ontario Creates.

Contents

Introduction: Welcome to Devil's Kettle

I didn't rush to the multiplex to see *Jennifer's Body* when it came out in 2009. The premise seemed fun enough — a popular teen girl gets possessed by a demon and wreaks havoc on her small Midwestern town as her best friend tries to stop her — but trailers weren't exactly tantalizing (or accurate), and reviews were as damned as Jennifer herself. But browsing one night at my local video store, I took a chance.

And what a treat! Why did people sleep on this? *Jennifer's Body* was hilarious, touching, dark as hell, and way queerer than I was used to for a mainstream movie that wasn't *about* queerness. "I thought it was pretty good," I would tell anyone who wrote it off. "Have you seen her in *Jennifer's Body*?" I'd ask anyone critical of the film's star, Megan Fox. And it seriously stuck with me. Over the next few years, I fell in love with horror, grew critical of how Hollywood treats women, and embraced my own queerness, and so *Jennifer's Body* spoke to me more and more as time went on. Every passing year saw me just a little more baffled at how little love it had gotten.

So many mid-budget horror films aimed at teens and starring the ingenue-du-jour fall flat, but *Jennifer's Body* is an emotionally satisfying look at female friendship, queer love, and gendered violence, all wrapped up in a package that's infused with horror film history. The film stands alone, but has notes of everything from *Carrie* to *An American Werewolf in London* to *The Lost Boys* to *Ginger Snaps*.

It takes a deft hand to balance humor and horror without sacrificing one or the other; the film walks that line expertly, finding the funny even in heartbreaking moments of violence between Fox's titular Jennifer Check and her best friend, Anita "Needy" Lesnicki, played by Amanda Seyfried, who wants to save the girl she loves — and all the innocents her BFF keeps ingesting too.

That *Jennifer's Body* is good — great, even — has everything and nothing to do with its failure. Taste is a funny thing, and it's inextricably linked to cultural contexts. Can quality be measured objectively? Is a film inherently good or bad and then subject to whether people respond appropriately to it? Whether they *get* it? Can art truly be produced "before its time" and waiting for us all to catch up?

"I remember watching it and thinking it was terrific. It was a really strong voice by a strong director. Smart, sharp characters. I liked the whole satanic possession by accident.

It was just a smart, clever film. Basically smarter than most of the stuff I was seeing," Toronto International Film Festival (TIFF) programmer Colin Geddes told me of his decision to program *Jennifer's Body* as part of Midnight Madness, the festival's genre-centric and fan-favorite midnight screening series, in 2009. He managed to appreciate a good film in the moment, and the premiere audience, who hung around for a Q&A at two a.m., seemed to agree.

So, what went wrong? Why, when *Jennifer's Body* moved into wide release, was it met with so little enthusiasm? Overlapping backlashes against screenwriter Diablo Cody and Megan Fox set it back from the get-go. Cody, a young stripper-turned-blogger-turned-screenwriter, was hot off her screenwriting Oscar win for sleeper hit *Juno*, which faced major pushback from conservatives and progressives alike almost overnight. Fox, meanwhile, got herself fired (or did she quit?) from Michael Bay's megahit *Transformers* franchise shortly after a public feud that coincided perfectly with the *Jennifer's Body* rollout. Those two separate pushbacks against Cody and Fox were among the many signs of an industry disturbingly primed to tear down the young women whose talents it chews up like Jennifer does a barbecue chicken.

But Hollywood has faced a dramatic reckoning since *Jennifer's Body* bombed at the box office. In 2017, after the *New York Times* published allegations of decades of sexual abuse by Harvey Weinstein, women, in Hollywood and beyond, flooded the internet with their own terrible #MeToo tales. The boys' club mentality of the film industry has also come under fire in the years since 2009, with film festivals making commitments to reach gender parity among the directors on their programming slates. The *Jennifer's Body* writer/director team of Diablo Cody and Karyn Kusama certainly stood out in 2009, especially in the male-dominated horror genre, but not enough to genuinely make it into the press cycle the way "50/50" initiatives have since. If anything, a female creative team may have still been seen as a liability rather than a mark of progress.

In contrast, ten years later, a reimagining of 1974's prototypical slasher classic *Black Christmas*, directed by Sophia Takal and written by Takal and April Wolfe, became a bit of a flashpoint for discussions of women in horror, with the *Los Angeles Times* calling it a "fiercely feminist slasher movie for the #MeToo era."[1] In 2018, a year earlier, *Halloween* actress Jamie Lee Curtis had linked the latest installment in that franchise to #MeToo as well.[2] As I watched this movement make its way to horror films, I thought back to *Jennifer's Body*: a story now tapped into the zeitgeist, with one character assaulted but finding agency in her newfound monstrosity and the other fighting to save someone she loves deeply.

Jennifer's Body grounds itself (and its more outrageous moments of supernatural fiction) in recognizable slices of teen life and the horrors of systemic misogyny in a way that gives it staying power. Even further, the ways in which *Jennifer's Body* was cast aside make its own themes of abuse, victim-blaming, and messy revenge all the more powerful — and "still socially relevant," to borrow a phrase from Jennifer herself.

4

"*Jennifer's Body* would kill if it came out today," I wrote in an article for *VICE*, unpacking how the film's themes would have been better received in the #MeToo era and how Megan Fox's career had been derailed by Michael Bay.[3] As the tenth anniversary approached, I was one of many culture writers revisiting *Jennifer's Body* as a #MeToo narrative that came too soon. It was a better-late-than-never backlash to the backlash.

But can we really reduce the rise of *Jennifer's Body* to its tenth anniversary just barely coinciding with #MeToo? Is everyone, as *Vox*'s Constance Grady put it, "just now starting to get on its level"?[4] To some degree, yes. The massive surge in appreciation has propelled the movie from niche cult object to international conversation starter. The film didn't change — we did.

We realized what we'd wanted all along. More stories from women, about women; complex stories filled with blood and laughter and friendship and betrayal. More nuanced queer stories. More stories that could engage with the monstrosity so recently exposed in the world.

Jennifer was waiting.

1

The Pieces of *Jennifer's Body*

"I specifically, my entire life, had dreamed of writing a horror movie. I'm a huge horror fan," Diablo Cody told Megan Fox during a filmed sit-down in 2019, coinciding with the tenth anniversary of *Jennifer's Body*.[1] "I always wanted to do something like that — a horror movie with a female protagonist and a female villain. And that was what I wrote," Cody told *Vox* in 2018. "People were enthusiastic about it. Nobody said to me, 'Oh, I don't know, after *Juno*, maybe you should do another high school comedy' or 'Maybe this is not the right project for you.' People were supportive."[2]

Cody wrote *Jennifer's Body* before *Juno* had even gone into production, she said at TIFF. "I had finished [writing] *Juno*, and we had the ball rolling on that project, and so I had some time to myself — i.e., no life — and I thought to myself,

Alright, well now what do I really want to do? What appeals to me? What would I want to see? And immediately, I thought a horror film. So, I just started writing this one just on spec, not knowing that there would be any success to come with *Juno*."[3]

Cody experienced a rapid rise to fame that's extremely rare for screenwriters. She'd been something of a dark horse with her 2007 sleeper hit; the irreverent indie comedy about the complexities of teen parenthood wasn't an obvious Oscar contender. But *Juno* had sharp dialogue and an uplifting, progressive message, along with a breakout role for its star, Elliot Page. Cody's Oscar win felt like a Hollywood Cinderella ending with a punk-feminist edge. And that success gave her an advantage when developing her next project.

With an executive producer credit on *Jennifer's Body*, Cody had an uncommon amount of creative control for a screenwriter, including having a say in selecting director Karyn Kusama. The two clicked, sharing a love of horror as well as a distinct vision for the film's central relationship. "It was so razor-sharp and funny and outrageous and scary, and, for me, it really spoke to the idea of toxic friendships between girls, particularly as teenagers," Kusama told me about her initial interest after reading the script. "That was sort of my way into the material and how I planned to explore it."

The two shared reference points for the film's tone and style, too, preferring warmth and color to the colder look of contemporaneous horror films like another 2009 Midnight Madness debut, the dystopian sci-fi vampire film *Daybreakers*. Cody and Kusama looked instead to the vivid colors used by people like horror legend Dario Argento and to tonally idio-syncratic classics like *A Nightmare on Elm Street*, *An American Werewolf in London*, and *The Howling* for inspiration.[4] While Cody had never before written a horror film, and Kusama had worked in indie drama then big-budget sci-fi with her debut feature *Girlfight* and follow-up *Æon Flux*, the two were clearly primed to dive into horror as fans with something to add to the genre.

Executive producer Mason Novick was on board from the jump. Novick had already been working with Cody for years, after coming across her blog, reportedly while looking for porn. He'd immediately connected with her writing and became her manager, and the two have worked together since.[5] Cody, née Brook Busey, now Brook Maurio, rose to internet fame with her blog chronicling her experiences as a stripper in Minneapolis. She published her memoir, *Candy Girl: A Year in the Life of an Unlikely Stripper*, a year before *Juno*'s release.

Novick was the one to propose Megan Fox for the role of Jennifer before Karyn Kusama had even been brought on as director, and no one else was ever seriously considered for the role once Fox was in the running. "She just had that . . . she had that *thing*," Novick told me, "the thing everyone was talking about. I could tell she was going to go supernova."

Hollywood is obviously full of talented and beautiful actresses, but "that thing" that Fox brought to the table was something else, something different and complicated and reflective of a lot of the issues *Jennifer's Body* is trying to unpack: Megan Fox was a hot actress gracing the covers of magazines and dominating entertainment headlines, but she also had an air of mystery and unattainability, and she was scorned for taking up too much space on the scene and rising "too quickly."

It's easy to compare Fox to Jennifer as a popular girl with a bad reputation. Jennifer brushes off come-ons from boys with a practiced insouciance, like she knows she's seen as a status symbol, not someone people are trying to actually make a connection with. "Just go ahead with the pitch," she says to her schoolmate, soon-to-be-devoured Colin, when he tries to ask her out. She's kept on a pedestal, and she knows it. She uses it to her advantage, but it has its drawbacks, from getting dirty looks and judgment from classmates to being targeted for abuse by men.

"You have mystique," Cody told Fox, when the actress asked her what it was about her that convinced Cody she "could play a psychopath that devours boys": "In this era of social media and people being completely accessible, it's rare. And old movie stars had mystique . . . So many of the actresses in your cohort, I could not imagine playing Jennifer, because they did not have the self-possessed, Ava Gardner–type quality that you have, and we just knew."[6]

Amanda Seyfried was perhaps a less obvious choice as Needy, the film's leading lady. She had the star power, certainly, with two simultaneous TIFF world premieres on deck that year, and roles in beloved projects like *Veronica Mars* and *Mean Girls*, as well as high-profile credits like *Mamma Mia!* But those roles, and her star persona, hadn't created the same fixed impression in the collective consciousness that Fox had. In *Veronica Mars*, she plays Lilly Kane, an entitled and popular girl murdered, her death to be avenged by her own best friend, the titular teen sleuth. In *Mean Girls*, she's the over-the-top "dumb blonde" of the queen-bee Plastics at a Midwestern high school. The two roles combined could have served in lieu of an audition tape for the role of Jennifer, but Seyfried's performance pushes against her best-known roles.

Kusama and Cody met with other actresses including Emma Stone, Lizzy Caplan, and Amanda Bynes while casting Needy,[7] before landing on Seyfried, who they realized "was clearly perfect for the part,"[8] and she offered a rich and layered performance, working beautifully opposite Fox.

Kusama came onboard not long after Fox, in the fall of 2008. Kusama, like Cody, had become one to watch following her first feature. Her indie darling *Girlfight* followed its 2000 premiere at Sundance by racking up awards there and at Cannes. It wasn't an easy road, though. Kusama had battled to get *Girlfight* produced, pressured by prospective producers to make her Latina protagonist white. She eventually found a suitable production team, with her $1 million budget provided personally by producer Maggie Renzi and her partner (Kusama's former mentor and fellow filmmaker) John Sayles.[9]

Her high-profile follow-up project ended up being 2005's *Æon Flux*. Written by Phil Hay — whom Kusama later married — and Matt Manfredi, the movie was an adaptation of Peter Chung's bizarre dystopian animated cult serial of the same name, which aired on MTV in the early '90s. It was to be a heady sci-fi pic, a kind of big-budget art film exploring love, the soul, and human cloning in a hermetic future society, with action set pieces shot with balletic choreography, starring Charlize Theron on the heels of her best actress Oscar win for 2003's *Monster*.

That movie never made it onto theater screens. After cutting the proposed production budget roughly in half, Paramount Pictures went through some restructuring, and the film was eventually taken from Kusama and edited into something unrecognizable. Among other changes, the sexuality of a gay character was excised, and intricately choreographed action scenes were chopped into frantic, high-octane junk.[10]

"The emotional core of things was always being questioned as sentimental, over-romantic, short of literally saying the words 'female' or 'feminine,'" Kusama told *BuzzFeed*. "Huge swatches of storyline, which gave the movie a kind of emotional weight, were completely removed."[11]

"It was a real baptism in the brutal logic of Hollywood. It came early on, so I had time to reflect on it. I received my indie darling moment and learned that it is fleeting," Kusama has said of the experience.[12]

After the commercial failure and artistic disappointment of *Æon Flux*, Kusama was happy to work on a project with Cody, whose success with *Juno* might free her from studio meddling.[13] And the two came up with a fresh and original story full of depth and social commentary.

Through Needy's narration and point of view, *Jennifer's Body* tells the story of Jennifer Check, a teen cheerleader who becomes possessed by a demon and preys on the teen boys at Devil's Kettle High. It's a story of teen friendship between girls, irreconcilable conflict, and romantic affection — "You're totally lesbigay," an astute if dismissive fellow student whispers to Needy, noticing her beaming at her friend as she watches her flag team routine from the bleachers.

But Jennifer's not just out for blood or chosen at random for a sacrifice. The indie rock band Low Shoulder picks her out of a crowd based on false and misogynistic assumptions about her sexuality. A hot and flirty teen like Jennifer must be merely a tease, and thus actually a virgin, they think, which is just what they need for a deal with the devil that will bring them fame and fortune. But Jennifer wasn't even, in her own words, "a backdoor virgin" when they picked her.

While the sacrifice of Jennifer's body works for the band — they rocket to a Maroon 5 level of success — Jennifer doesn't stay dead: she comes back a succubus, a demon feasting on boys to stay vital, only to be killed by her best friend, whose ultimate sacrifice (and presumably her ravings about satanic rockers) land her in the psych ward.

Jennifer's Body plays with genre conventions, flaunting its horror bona fides, smoothly and intelligently picking and choosing when to subvert them and make its own mark. Like *Carrie*, it depicts a manifestation of feminine rage in the face of genuine abuses and gendered injustice. Like *The Lost Boys*, it explores high school cliques and the teenaged need to find and maintain human bonds by framing them through the threat of monstrosity and losing yourself to something too powerful to control. Like *An American Werewolf in London* and millennial werewolf classic *Ginger Snaps*, it links monstrous transformation to more human relationships that morph and evolve and threaten to break during developmental milestones.

But *Jennifer's Body* diverges from the dominant flavor of horror movies of the era. From 2004 to 2010, the *Saw* franchise released a title per year at Halloween. The films, often dubbed "torture porn," were part of a cycle of nihilistic horror titles fascinated by the randomness of death and violence, most easily attributed to a post-9/11 state of fear and desensitization to images of the so-called War on Terror and atrocities like the torture of inmates by American soldiers in Iraq at Abu Ghraib prison. *Saw*'s fingerprints are also all over the *Hostel* and *Final Destination* franchises and 2007's darkly bizarre *I Know Who Killed Me*, among others.

While steering clear of anything we could call torture porn or a nihilistic reflection of the death and violence of the Bush years, Cody did insert her own brief nod to 9/11, as she describes on *Jennifer's Body*'s audio commentary. Jennifer's first victim is an exchange student dismissively referred to only as "Ahmet from India." Before luring him into the woods to kill him, Jennifer asks him if his host family knows he's alive following the bar fire. He shakes his head. "Does anyone know you're alive?" she goes on. The wording is intentionally broad, Cody says, pointing to the xenophobic dehumanization of immigrant communities after the crimes of a tiny group of terrorists were projected onto entire populations of people.

No one in that Midwestern town really knew or cared that Ahmet was alive to begin with. Not in any meaningful way.

(Another brief nod to the general weirdness of America's response to the national tragedy comes when Jennifer, hoping to hook up with Low Shoulder front man Nikolai, buys him tacky red, white, and blue 9/11 tribute shooters, one of the bar's signature drinks, served in twos to grimly commemorate the Twin Towers.)

Jennifer's Body plays a precarious game here, depicting offensive stereotypes — Jennifer comparing the smell of sex to Thai food or suggesting Needy find "a Chinese chick to buff your situation" when she sees her chipped and dirty fingernails — without fully reckoning with them. The film doesn't exactly endorse Jennifer's behavior, even before her transformation, but it does allow these lines to play at least in part for laughs in ways that can be uncomfortable. Putting these lines in Jennifer's mouth (or words like "retarded" in Nikolai's) creates some necessary distance from their offensiveness — it's not the film saying these things but rather the edgy characters in the film — as does the parodic treatment of small-town American xenophobia, but it adds a cultural bleakness that doesn't feel fully explored.

The generic horror markers in *Jennifer's Body* were less bleak but no less recognizable. The film is told from Needy's perspective, as she narrates from the confines of a psychiatric correctional facility. Needy's narration immediately evokes tropes of madwomen and of unreliable narrators, dating back cinematically at least as far as Robert Wiene's 1920 German expressionist masterpiece *The Cabinet of Dr. Caligari*, in which a famous twist ending reveals that the protagonist narrator is institutionalized and recounting a fictional story starring his fellow asylum patients and their doctors. By establishing that Needy is locked away and dangerous at the outset, Cody and Kusama tap into a well-established tradition that forces us to wonder if the entire saga is all in her mind. But, of course, that's complicated by the theme of women being underestimated, exploited, and disbelieved that runs through the film as a whole.

"There's a grand tradition of narrators in the mental hospital," says Cody, on the *Jennifer's Body* commentary track. "And there's a grand tradition of women in mental hospitals who shouldn't be there," adds Kusama.

The film hinges on us siding with our protagonist at least a bit. This lets Cody and Kusama play with both gender and horror tropes. Our very first introduction to Needy is destabilizing, to say the least. She viciously attacks a nurse who is, as far as we can tell, just concerned for her well-being and making sure she's getting enough nutrients from her Toast'em breakfast pastries. She's getting fan mail for crimes we aren't fully aware of yet. She talks about her imprisonment with a measured cynicism that hints she's seen some shit, all while walking around her cell in cute bunny slippers, surrounded by stuffed animals and a framed photo of her high school sweetheart. Cody and Kusama are winking at us, offering an ironic and nihilistic tone that skews our expectations away from any straightforward narrative. Needy is the innocent child and the menacing inmate all at once. She's loved and admired, but also feared and misunderstood. We can't immediately get a good foothold on what we're watching.

We soon also see what Needy's been through, or what she tells us she's been through. Much like Jennifer, Needy is hero, villain, victim, and aggressor all at once. We can't just trust in authority figures who have decided that Needy belongs in isolation under constant supervision. Something's off, even if Needy is, as her chart suggests, "a kicker."

Cody and Kusama train us to question what we're seeing. They keep dropping hints that something about Needy's version of events is a little far-fetched — beyond the whole demonic possession thing. Even before Jennifer's transformation, and our first introduction to the occult, Needy describes an almost psychic bond. She and Jennifer sense each other's presence with what seems like supernatural precognition. This is visually reinforced by a lighting effect when they're holding hands at Melody Lane, the bar where Jennifer is taken by Low Shoulder. As they let go, marks left on both their hands look just a little too bright, like a flash of energy pointing to a fantastical connection between them.

Is Needy recounting something real, or has she mythologized her relationship with Jennifer in the retelling? What we're seeing could, hypothetically, be a representation of her emotional reality — sometimes growing apart from someone you care deeply about can *feel* like they've been possessed. Her boyfriend Chip openly worries about her mental health and suggests she see the "school shrink." And if she is imagining things, how else might the narrative be her creation? Ultimately, the truth is that Needy is being gaslit, that she's part of the "grand tradition" of women institutionalized on false premises.

Needy as madwoman-narrator is one of many throwbacks that play with our expectations, mixing familiarity and surprise. The film offers gender-flipped takes on formulas seen in vampire films like *The Lost Boys* and werewolf films like *An American Werewolf in London*, asking: What does it mean to change and grow apart? How can monstrosity symbolize a rift in a relationship and the challenges of growing up? Both of those films dig into specifically male relationships, with a kind of built-in machismo driving the symbolism and metaphors of interpersonal dynamics. *Jennifer's Body* plays with these same themes and shares the use of horrific (and nonconsensual) transformation to tell a story grounded in more feminine dynamics. It goes beyond surface-level references to tackle what it means more broadly to be a teen girl in a world hostile to teen girls. What if monstrosity is what's projected onto survivors of abuse? What if trauma can't be contained?

Not that there's anything wrong with surface-level references. It's hard to escape comparisons to *Prom Night* and, especially, *Carrie* when you put a supernaturally powerful, vengeful teen girl in a white prom dress, and *Jennifer's Body* plays the parallel skillfully (even if Jennifer and Needy are attending a spring formal and not technically prom). Jennifer offers another throwback to *Carrie* when she asks Needy for a tampon on the pretense that her bestie seems like she's "pluggin'," a nod to Carrie's humiliation when her schoolmates threw tampons and pads at her, chanting "plug it up." That said, Jennifer's request is casual and offhanded, poking fun more at the very concept of PMS (which she'd earlier dismissed as an invention of the "boy-run media") than at Needy or her menstruation itself.

It's a moment for Megan Fox to shine and show off her acting skills, too, as Jennifer and Needy trade barbs as they face off in an abandoned pool near the end of the film. Here, Fox lays bare Jennifer's vulnerability, countering Needy's claim of insecurity with an unconvincing "How could I ever be insecure? I was the Snowflake Queen!" This piece of dialogue would have been so easy to blow, either overplaying the sad desperation or leaning too hard into the silliness of high school hierarchies. Instead, Fox imbues the moment with genuine pathos. "Yeah, two years ago, when you were socially relevant," Needy bites back, knowing exactly how to get under Jennifer's skin. It's an important role reversal, where Needy exploits Jennifer's very real insecurities, whether Jennifer admits them or not.

We can't help but empathize with Jennifer and the sense of loss she feels as her social position changes. The tenuous power of being the Snowflake Queen might be the last vestige of her adolescent, explicitly feminine self-worth. Even in her possessed form, when she has raw murderous power, it's the lapsed title of "Snowflake Queen," symbolically so delicate and fleeting, that reveals a chink in her armor. As

Jennifer palpably shrinks before us, Needy pushes harder, calling out her need for laxatives to stay skinny. It's no coincidence that the possessed Jennifer's physical beauty is one of the first things to fade when she's gone too long without a meal. Whether human, or monster, she's been forced to define herself by status symbols she can't control. We're seeing her at a crossroads. Fox puts a devastatingly human face on that process, brings relatability to monstrosity, without compromising either the comedy or horror of the moment.

For all the genre boxes *Jennifer's Body* checks, it's hardly an exercise in blind reverence, and that's one of the film's great strengths. Nearly every genre signifier is a loose thread. The more you pull at it, the more the rules of the game start to unravel and expose how thoughtful Cody and Kusama are about conventions, questioning who is a monster and who is a victim, what collective grief means, how teen sexuality is punished or valorized, and more.

One prime example of this is how the two play with the idea of Needy as the "Final Girl" of the film. Carol Clover, who coined the term, calls the Final Girl the "tortured survivor" and "hero-victim" rather than the hero.[14] The Final Girl makes it to the end of the film and eventually takes down the killer. "The practiced viewer distinguishes her from her friends minutes into the film. She is the Girl Scout, the bookworm, the mechanic. Unlike her girlfriends (and Marion Crane) she is not sexually active," she says, referring to Alfred Hitchcock's *Psycho* and its first victim, adding that the Final Girl is often boyish or at least not as feminine as her friends.[15]

Clover was talking about American slasher films of the 1970s and '80s specifically, but her concept of the Final Girl has stuck around and informed horror scholarship as well as horror films themselves. Movies like 1996's *Scream*, 2011's *You're Next*, and 2011's *The Cabin in the Woods* all play with the trope and try, like Clover, to unpack what it means to be a Final Girl. 2015 was an especially strong year for Final Girl discourse within horror movies, with the darkly self-aware *Final Girl* and the more tongue-in-cheek *The Final Girls* both competing for eyeballs and butts in seats.

Needy is *almost* a textbook Final Girl. She survives Jennifer's killing spree and successfully faces off with her despite skepticism from her own boyfriend, Chip, who doesn't expect anything more than "high school evil" from Jennifer. But if we make our way down Clover's checklist, Needy subverts the trope in a few fun ways. True to form, Amanda Seyfried isn't particularly believable as the plain Jane to Megan Fox's hot girl — like classic Final Girls played by Vera Miles, Jamie Lee Curtis, and Neve Campbell, she's been cast in plenty of conventionally attractive roles and is just dressed down for the part. But Needy isn't a Hollywood teen movie cardboard cutout either. She can feel inadequate next to Jennifer even if she's pretty, and be the nerd without sacrificing partying, having sex, and dressing up to go out.

A lot of the ways we're trained to see Needy as unfeminine are projected onto her. We're typically told that brainy girls like Needy are somehow above the fray. They're "not like other girls." The film pushes back against that, though, by showing us the social pressure that enables this sexist pigeon-holing. Jennifer looking sexy is perceived as normal, and Needy's narration suggests that Jennifer's rules for looking cute are what hold her back from dressing more like Jennifer. She even gets pushback from Chip when she does get dressed up to go out. "Those jeans are hella low. I can almost see your front butt," he says. There's an obvious tone of disapproval, but also an implication that this isn't who Needy is. That revealing clothes and makeup are for other girls, and that this doesn't conform to who she's supposed to be. All of this despite the fact that they're her jeans, from her closet. This is at least a part of who she is.

None of those things are necessarily or inherently feminine, but they're the kind of social norms that pass for femininity in American culture and in the rules that Clover identifies. Needy is a complex human person, though, and those traits are all part of a much deeper character who isn't any more or less a young woman than anyone else. She fits the profiles of various types but can't be reduced to just one.

Maybe the biggest subversion of the Final Girl trope is that Needy isn't a virgin, even at the start of the film. She and Chip, by all appearances, have a healthy, active sex life. They have sex within the film, and Chip makes reference to buying "more condoms," suggesting the two have run out at some point. Still, they're a monogamous, loving couple, which conforms to the Final Girl's broader sense of "purity," albeit in an updated, slightly more sex-positive way. The Final Girl as virgin is probably the most outdated part of the formula. *Scream* did away with it in 1996 while explicitly framing it as a broken "rule." But still, in *Scream* and later slashers, the Final Girl is usually at least monogamous, saving herself for the right guy. True to that, the more by-the-book Needy is still set up in contrast to rebellious Jennifer, who has had multiple sexual partners. It's true that Jennifer's killing spree could have been prevented if she'd been a virgin — though, of course, that wouldn't have saved *her*. The rules in this situation are literally diabolical, and the dichotomy between pure and impure is fundamentally not the problem. The problem is how sex is used, abused, warped, and mapped onto people's reputations to create an arbitrary, deeply sexist moral order.

Beyond challenging the Final Girl trope, the low-key, normcore depiction of Needy's sex life is oddly refreshing. It fits into the broader treatment of the teen experience in the film, which touches on everything from the mundane, everyday experiences of being a kid, to the pressures of growing up, to the sometimes-dangerous reality of being a girl in a misogynistic world.

Jennifer's Body plays with genre conventions throughout, but it also has so much to say about existing in America as a teen girl in the early 2000s. The scariest part of this horror film is not the demonic possession or (literal) man-eating, but a violent patriarchal world that sees girls as disposable, as tools to get ahead. *Jennifer's Body* engages, head-on, with the world we live in, warts and all. Warts especially.

2

"The Movie I Wanted to Make"

Authorial intent is a tricky beast. Everything that's in a film was put there, but that doesn't always mean it's there intentionally. "Queering" of non-queer films and TV shows is a perfect example — fans spot romantic undertones in relationships and markers of identity that creators never necessarily intended (and are sometimes even hostile to). Who owns the meaning of a given film? Who has final say?

I've long subscribed to the idea that when a film and its filmmaker disagree, the film gets final say. Or as the late Canadian film critic and scholar Peter Harcourt would say, "Between the film and the filmmaker, trust the film." If intended subtext doesn't come across, it's not really there. And if unintended subtext informs how you read the film, then it's part of the film. But that doesn't mean that films and filmmakers *have* to disagree. Sometimes a film and its filmmaker are in perfect accord, while studios, critics, and audiences are the ones with other ideas, as was sadly the case with *Jennifer's Body*.

In one early, telling moment during the TIFF press conference, Fox hinted at the tasteless and ultimately dishonest marketing to come, saying in a mocking tone, "If I were to use my talking points from the studio, I would call it 'a sexy thriller with a wicked sense of humor,' but I think that it's a comedy with horror elements."[1] Even at TIFF, where excitement over *Jennifer's Body* was as high as it would get for a decade, a sense of foreboding managed to creep in, as though the industry wasn't ready to properly handle something this nuanced.

A lot changed at 20th Century Fox from the time *Jennifer's Body* was greenlit to the night of its premiere. The film was one of the last projects to come out of the short-lived Fox Atomic, a genre-focused, youth-skewing imprint of 20th Century Fox launched in 2006 with the horror film *Turistas*, about a bunch of hot young backpackers in Brazil getting embroiled in a nightmarish organ-harvesting scheme.

The early buzz around Atomic was that it would sidestep traditional Hollywood marketing and hit teens right where they lived online. The youthful mini studio would target platforms like custom fan sites, Myspace, virtual community *Second Life*, and then-fledgling video site YouTube. There was a whole print strategy, too, with tie-in comic books written by industry heavyweights that went an extra step from novelizing screenplays and actually filled in blanks and expanded movie worlds.[2] Some of those early comic titles included

28 Days Later: The Aftermath and *The Hills Have Eyes: The Beginning*, both timed to coincide with the releases of their respective high-profile franchise films, *28 Weeks Later* and *The Hills Have Eyes 2*.

However well or poorly executed the original idea may have been, the belief that millennial viewers might be better served and more accessible by means other than playing standard trailer fare at the multiplex proved true. Why not create word-of-mouth through more carefully curated guerrilla marketing techniques that might better pique the interests of a whole generation of people with disposable income and a tendency to socialize online?

The reality wasn't quite so rosy, though. The company almost immediately showed signs of strain. At the start of 2008, just barely over a year after launch, 20th Century Fox and Fox Searchlight took over marketing operations for Atomic.[3] Then in 2009, Fox shut down Atomic for good. The last few remaining titles were migrated to 20th Century Fox and Fox Searchlight, which oversaw their post-production and marketing. These included the comedies *I Love You, Beth Cooper* and *Post Grad* along with, you guessed it, *Jennifer's Body*.[4]

It's tempting to see this timeline and assume too many cooks spoiled the marketing stew for *Jennifer's Body*, as the film was shuffled around in what must have been a chaotic game of telephone between marketing execs. But Megan Fox's comments about studio notes reflect a pretty consistent (and consistently tone-deaf) rollout leaning heavily on her sex-symbol status. There's no hint of the film's thematic preoccupations to be found, notably its commentary on gender. It's odd, to say the least, that the strategy was to side-step so much of what makes *Jennifer's Body* actually worth watching and warp it into something nearly unrecognizable.

Take the film's official trailer, for instance.

We open on Jennifer swimming, naked, with quick cuts to her walking through crowded school halls in slow motion, carefree. The hallway strut sequence has become shorthand for popular mean-girl dominance, already the subject of a send-up in teen movie parody *Not Another Teen Movie* almost a decade before in 2001. More quick cuts, and Jennifer's looking at herself in a vanity mirror. Text on-screen reads: "In every school, there's one girl every girl wants to be friends with. And every guy would die for." We see Needy's loyal boyfriend Chip complaining that "you always do what Jennifer tells you to do," as Needy is told (not invited) to go out with her bestie tonight. "Wear something cute, okay?" Jennifer reminds Needy. From there, we see Jennifer preying on boys who lust after her, with the tease of a girl-on-girl kiss thrown in for good measure.

Jennifer's monstrosity is front and center, which makes sense, but all of its context is rewritten into something way less interesting than what Cody and Kusama actually pulled off. Jennifer's popular-mean-girl-cheerleader packaging is worth thinking about, but it's not inherently tied to or even just a symptom of her possession, which is the trailer's implication. The film deliberately establishes her character before Jennifer is turned: she's bossy, dismissive, a bit self-centered. In short, she's human: neither a "perfect victim" nor a deserving target.

Needy's assurances to Chip in the trailer ("It's just that I like the same things that she likes") are unconvincing, suggesting a familiar tale of a nerdy loser plucked from obscurity by a popular girl. It's a variation on *Heathers, Clueless, The Craft, She's All That, Jawbreaker, 13 Going on 30, Mean Girls*, and plenty of other teen classics. It's a fun trope with lots of potential, but you won't find it in *Jennifer's Body*. Needy and Jennifer have a genuine, ongoing bond, a lifelong friendship. There's a power imbalance from the start, but Needy never comes off just as Jennifer's lapdog. Needy's loyalty to her best friend supersedes a date night with her boyfriend because they have a longer history than her (other) high school romance, not because she's desperate to be one of the cool girls.

But the trailer's framing suggests a film about teen-girl manipulation, jealousy over boys, and Megan Fox's body served up hot for hungry male eyes. One of the film's ubiquitous posters echoed this misdirection. Fox gazes into the camera from the front of a classroom, wearing a short plaid skirt and heels. She hugs school books to her chest, with a severed human hand just visible, protruding from the desk she's perched on. In another version, she's seated at a different desk, the human hand instead sticking out of her backpack. In both versions, the blackboard behind her reads "Hell yes!" The image antithetically evokes fantasies of both the school teacher and the schoolgirl, with a cursory nod to the maneater.

If the marketing missed its mark, critics didn't course correct as the film rolled out, often missing the same story beats and themes left out of the trailer and posters. For the most part, reviews ignored the rewarding depth and nuance of the horror-comedy.

The A.V. Club called *Jennifer's Body* an "excruciating teen horror-comedy" and declared the film "clever for its own sake, a showy piece of writing that doesn't have that all-important ballast of sincerity."[5] This was the dominant view among critics on the story of a teen girl turned into a monster. Some focused on Megan Fox's perceived lack of talent — a baffling attitude in retrospect, as the actress brings a rich complexity to the tragedy of Jennifer Check. Others were annoyed at the slangy flippancy of the script. And some took issue with the film's tone, wanting more or less of either the horror or comedy, depending on the reviewer.

These reviews were written amidst a simmering revolt against Megan Fox and a rather sudden backlash against Diablo Cody.

Fox's sex-symbol status had been used as evidence of her vapidity and dumb luck for years before *Jennifer's Body*, and her genuine talent had been erased in predictable ways, over-written by her physicality in the *Transformers* films. She was understandably tired of being objectified and reduced to her looks in the action films and was upfront about it in interviews. "I didn't have to bend over a bike, which was nice," she said of working with Kusama, who, as a woman, could more easily relate to her on set.[6] That willingness to talk about her own experiences was also punished, though, most dramatically on the eve of the *Jennifer's Body* premiere, when an article was published in which she called her *Transformers* director,

Michael Bay, a tyrant on set and casually compared him to Adolf Hitler.[7] Her baseless reputation as little more than a pretty face was now compounded by collective outrage at her perceived ingratitude to her benefactor.

As for Cody, as the Associated Press's Erin Carlson noted, "Being the most famous stripper-turned-screenwriter in the world isn't always as pleasant as it may sound."[8] Pushback against Cody was common enough during the film's rollout that it was mentioned frequently in reviews. *Slashfilm*'s Peter Sciretta opened his rare positive review with a nod to the Cody backlash and cautioned, "If you hate Cody, I doubt *Jennifer's Body* will do much to change your mind. There are sure to be a lot of naysayers with a vocal agenda who will likely never give this film a real chance."[9]

It's sadly predictable that a young, outspoken woman striking gold on her first outing would invite some amount of scorn, as Cody did. Her politics were being criticized from all directions, so that her feminist cred was overlooked or even erased by some and seen as too radical by others. It was a no-win situation, compounded by a sense that her spunky teen heroine was out of step with reality. Juno and her friends' use of Cody's made-up slang was initially hailed as charming and quirky but recast as obnoxious incredibly quickly, with online snark taking the screenwriter to task for conspicuous lines like "honest to blog."

Jennifer telling Needy to "move on dot org" at one point in *Jennifer's Body* has a certain *Juno* flavor, along with other Codyisms: the underage Jennifer plays "Hello Titty" with a bartender to get drinks, quips about PMS being "invented by the boy-run media," tells soon-to-be-victim Colin that he gives her "such a wetty." She greets Needy with the playfully crass "where's it at, Monistat?" Hot boys are "salty morsels," and a rock band front man earns the upgraded "extra salty" label. A jealous person is "Jell-O," or "lime green Jell-O" if you want to cut deeper. Uncool behavior gets you "crossed out." Also like *Juno*, *Jennifer's Body* tells a story of a teen girl coping with a bodily transformation she didn't ask for with a similarly irreverent tone. It's hard not to believe some amount of cynical Diablo Cody fatigue spiked the overall reception to *Jennifer's Body*. "At the time I was very aware of people's desire for me to fail, so I felt like a lot of the reviews were informed by that," Cody told *BuzzFeed* in 2018. "It's less a truthful analysis of your art than it is a schadenfreude meter."[10]

But even if we brush off critics and audiences approaching *Jennifer's Body* with their minds made up about its star and screenwriter, there's a clear disconnect between the finished film and its marketing and reception. Specifically, there is what I'd diagnose as a refusal to engage with the film on anything even resembling its own terms. Which brings us back to authorial intent and the movie Diablo Cody and Karyn Kusama actually made versus the imaginary movie reflected in trailers and bad reviews. In 2018, Diablo Cody stood by the film, telling *Vox*'s Emily VanDerWerff that she loved how the film turned out, and "there's nothing I would change about the movie, and I have zero regrets about the experience."[11]

So, yes, when a film and its filmmaker disagree, the film gets final say, but what about when they do agree? If no one's actually listening to *either* the film or its filmmakers, then what?

"It was marketed to an audience I didn't make the movie for, which was very problematic," Karyn Kusama said in a 2019 *Nylon* interview.[12] Kusama has been pretty consistently frank about how completely mishandled the film's marketing was. But unlike with *Æon Flux*, she has been steadfast in standing by the finished product as her creative vision, and one she, like Cody, remains proud of: "The movie was really the movie I wanted to make and the movie that Diablo Cody wrote. In regards to its marketing, it was an epic misstep and they sold it to boys instead of to the girls who it was written for, and by, and about. They shifted the emphasis to boys based on Megan Fox's sex appeal."[13]

The question of who films are "for" was a big part of the critical response to *Jennifer's Body* at the time and has become a major part of its cultural resurrection. Roger Ebert, in a now nearly infamous review, called *Jennifer's Body* "*Twilight* for boys," referencing the much-maligned (though fantasti-cally successful) adaptation of Stephenie Meyer's young adult novels about a teen girl who falls in love with a vampire.[14] The first *Twilight* film (directed and written by women) hit cinemas just a year before *Jennifer's Body*.

It's an interesting comparison, especially coming from the legendary critic who was actually a lot more open to what both *Jennifer's Body* and *Twilight* were up to than many of his peers, showing some degree of respect and empathy for both films' fans, even while missing the mark on the former's target audience.

If *Jennifer's Body* suffered by being mismarketed to boys rather than girls, *Twilight* stands as a sad, if incredibly lucrative and popular, monument to the sexist attitudes that Hollywood both perpetuates and responds to when a media franchise is made for and marketed to girls and women. The vampire saga received mixed reviews but became a cultural lightning rod, the butt of jokes about vapid youth and overwrought feminine sentimentality.

The romance-horror-fantasy series, while trafficking in tropes that can hardly be called empowering to its own young heroine, Bella (played by Kristen Stewart in the film adaptations), didn't deserve anywhere near as much scorn as it received (nor did the brilliant Stewart, who suffered her own sexist backlash). I wouldn't go as far as to say it was the *Jennifer's Body* of 2008, but I also wouldn't hold it against anyone else if they did. The two are, to some degree, different sides of the same coin.

Negative reviews tended to disparage the teen audiences attracted to *Twilight* as much as they disparaged the film itself, treating them as an amorphous horde (sometimes explicitly labeled as such)[15] of "giddy," "swooning" girls[16] enamored of the cute boys on-screen if they put their phones down long enough to look up.[17] And you'd be hard pressed to find a late-night comedy host who didn't crack jokes about sparkly vampires in the months that followed *Twilight*'s release.

So, with that in mind, it's entirely possible that *Jennifer's Body* would still have bombed even if it had been marketed to the right group: mocking or dismissing the things teen girls love is sadly the norm and not the exception. Its lack of a built-in fandom (like the *Twilight Saga*'s) didn't help its odds, and even a savvy marketing strategy would have required a receptive market, including critics and a broader pop culture ecosystem willing to give it a fair shake. Was 2009 really the year for queer teen girls to break out into the mainstream, for instance? Would a close-up of Needy's hand ripping off Jennifer's BFF necklace have meant more if watched in that appropriate context? Would the heartbreak registering in Jennifer's eyes at such a symbolic rupture have landed?

What if the trailer had focused not just on friendship, but feminism? Jennifer as victim of patriarchal violence is instantly recognizable today, with the #MeToo movement having shifted the conversation, but if the film's reviews are any indication, it wasn't particularly noteworthy then. At least not to the tastemakers. I have to assume the sight of a creepy van, with young men luring a teen girl to her death in the woods would have been impactful to women of any age watching the film, certainly more than it was to the "boy-run media," who didn't even mention it in their reviews. The power of #MeToo, after all, came from the sense of a dark secret being spoken aloud and in community. That women found recognition and validation in no longer hiding their shared, systemic trauma, in their common lived experiences, finds its parallel when Jennifer confides in her best friend about her murder. The sacrifice scene was part of a much larger conversation that didn't break into the mainstream until many years later.

When I spoke to Karyn Kusama, she added that gender behind the camera also made the studio's strategies sting that much more: "This happens to men all the time. I'm not saying I'm alone. But because there were women at the center of the creative team, and of the very story we were trying to get out there into the theaters, it felt like there was a hostility against it that was a little more charged and personal."

Also charged and personally hurtful was one line of criticism that came up a few times in the press, straightwashing the queer love at the center of *Jennifer's Body*. Straightwashing usually happens within a film itself, as when Paramount removed *Æon Flux*'s queer storyline, but in this case, it was telegraphed onto *Jennifer's Body* after the fact, denying the queerness that *did* appear on-screen. It was effectively the opposite of queering and invited a justified ire — we have enough straight representation in pop culture that to erase what little queer representation does end up on our screens feels like a slap in the face. When critics treated a kiss between Jennifer and Needy as a ploy to titillate male viewers, calling it "apropos of nothing"[18] or "calculated eroticism,"[19] Kusama, who is herself queer, was understandably unimpressed.

"If there was anything that was sort of profoundly sad for me about the process of releasing the movie, it was to hear from often female critics that I was 'adopting the male gaze,'" she told me. "I chafe at anyone who tells me whose gaze I am adopting beyond my own. But that I somehow would do this for the pleasure of boys or men in the audience is insane . . . The queer content of the film was something that we very much wanted to explore and protect, and so it was sad to see it dismissed."

The kiss comes at a pivotal moment in *Jennifer's Body*. Needy's suspicions are all but confirmed, and she is ready to confront Jennifer, who has camped out in her bed waiting for her. Needy, who at first accuses Jennifer of the crimes they both know she has committed, leans into this moment of affection even while her guard is all the way up. That Jennifer can be this disarming, in this precise moment, means a lot. Suddenly, the depth of Jennifer and Needy's bond makes sense. They are lovers. Or at least some kind of romantic love exists between them. To misinterpret this moment as pandering to straight male fantasy is to give up on *Jennifer's Body* altogether.

This is yet another instance of the film and its filmmakers being perfectly in sync, despite a dominant narrative singing a different tune. Cody and Kusama, as well as Amanda Seyfried and Megan Fox, convey a sense of romantic love and yearning quite clearly — for anyone receptive to that kind of thing, at the very least — long before Needy and Jennifer lock lips. The kiss that eventually comes, after Needy has discovered Jennifer's secret, functions as a kind of direct and explicit confirmation of what has been only barely contained in the film's subtext, through prolonged and suggestive glances, casual flirtation and some rather overt musical cues. It really is disheartening that in a movie about demonic possession, it's the existence of bisexual teen girls that would be treated as outlandish. We can suspend our disbelief at Jennifer's levitation, but that a kiss between two girls could be anything but a performance of a straight male fantasy was a bridge too far, for some. Would Needy and Jennifer's bisexuality have been recognized for what it is if the whole film were judged as a story for teen girls? Or if viewers had been more empathetic to the film's characters, regardless of perceived authorial intent? It's difficult to deny the sincerity on-screen as Needy struggles with her feelings. It's not particularly titillating or erotic to watch her pull away, fearful but still full of affection. It's moving and powerful, though.

I have more to say on this point in the chapters that follow, but for now, suffice it to say that the straightwashing of *Jennifer's Body* provides one of the most clear-cut examples of a failure on the part of critics. We can talk about taste and subjectivity until the end of time, but this was an instance of rejecting the explicit reality on-screen in favor of using a deeply problematic, heteronormative lens: when two young women kiss in a romantic setting, the default critical position shouldn't be "how might this *not* be queer?"

The assumption that *Jennifer's Body* was pandering to the presumed horniness of teen boys rather than reflecting the experience of queer girls didn't come from nowhere, of course, as the trailers and other marketing materials make clear. Kusama has described a proposed marketing strategy to have Megan Fox host an amateur porn website to hype the film in what I'd charitably call an unconventional way.[20] The idea was both tastelessly exploitative of sex workers who have nothing to do with the film and disturbingly complicit in sexualizing a teenaged character. Kusama was predictably not impressed. When I asked her about it, she didn't mince words. "I really had to take a deep breath and come face to face with how deeply fucked up this world really is, because it was so insulting to Megan. It was so insulting to the film, to all the women who worked on the film and fucking created the film," she said. "Now that I look back on it, I wonder if it was just a way to say, 'In case you were wondering, we don't value you, and we just want you to be sure.' And so, it was hostile."

Diablo Cody has described a similar, if slightly less over-the-top, experience coming from test audiences in one incident that marked her enough that she held onto the review card submitted by one test audience member: "They said, 'What would you improve about this film?' And the kid wrote, 'Needs more boobs,' and spelled boobs b-e-w-b-s."[21]

Test audiences are hardly neutral ways to measure the potential success of a film. From the basic reality that we don't always know how to unpack, let alone articulate, how or why a film is connecting with us or not, to the difficult feat of assembling a test audience that matches the target audience, it's hard to justify altering an artistic vision based on test audience questionnaires. And if a certain demographic is asking for more bewbs, it's certainly fair to ask whose voices are being privileged in the studio's audience selection and whose voices are driving the studio's response. In short, if the film wasn't made for the kid demanding gratuitous nudity, why was his opinion solicited at all?

In the end, Diablo Cody offered a solid summary of how their authorial vision got lost on the way to the multiplex:

"People don't like women with big mouths, and there were a lot of them on that project. So, you know, let's chalk it up to misogyny."[22]

3

"Hell Is a Teenage Girl"

At its core, *Jennifer's Body* is about a teen female friendship, the fluid boundaries of that relationship, and what happens when it's challenged. Horror is often used to metaphorize all kinds of grounded, human realities, and it does a disservice to film history to pretend that thematic depth somehow elevates the genre, but *Jennifer's Body* does elevate the often-shallow depictions of teens — and especially teen girls — in pop culture more broadly.

Teen comedies and horror movies both are pretty male-dominated behind the camera, and we've ended up with mostly cookie-cutter girls. But not on Cody and Kusama's watch. There's no straightforward girl-power anthem to be had here, nor is Needy or Jennifer an outright villain. They're complex, and their relationship is too. "Hell is a teenage girl," says

ne single character — but in Fox's case, her
acter Mikaela Banes is notably smart. She's
e edges, having been raised by an ex-con, but
echanic around, and she's depicted as confi-
er intelligence throughout. But she's styled,
ot to capitalize on her hotness, overshadowing
well, character, in the same way that her sex
lattened the mainstream perception of Fox as a
a performer.

ht should be obvious, and her ability to imbue
th the very complexity she was denied is espe-
ng to watch as she plays Jennifer Check. Her flir-
Nikolai at Melody Lane is one of the first hints
lity masked by a facade of confidence that blends
g personality with the reality that she's still inse-
play your instruments really, super good," she says
smirking uncomfortably, like she already knows
but can't stop yet. The scene is incredibly sincere
s on the heels of Jennifer acting like she owns the
— and pulling that off too. It's bewildering to think
l watch Fox in moments like this and assume she's
but thoughtful and skilled at her craft.

learned that being a celebrity is like being a sacrificial
t some point, no matter how high the pedestal that
t you on, they're going to tear you down," Fox told
Iirschberg in the *New York Times Magazine* the year of
'*s Body*'s release. "I created a character as an offering for
rifice. I'm not willing to give my true self up . . . When I

44

Needy in the film's opening line, in voiceover, telegraphing
the toxicity and trauma that's about to unfold.

"If a guy wrote a movie with the line 'hell is a teenage
girl,' I would reject that," Cody has said. "But I'm allowed to
say it because I was one. I think the fact that we were a female
creative team gave us permission to make observations about
some of the more toxic aspects of female friendship."[1]

The tragedy of *Jennifer's Body* is as much the deteriorating
friendship between Jennifer and Needy as it is the deaths
of the boys Jennifer kills or the crime committed against
her. Being a teenager is weird and complicated, and when
Kusama says the concept of toxic female friendship attracted
her to the film, it's easy to see why. Jennifer and Needy both
get something out of each other, but we're seeing strain on
a relationship that dates back to early childhood. Jennifer's
flippancy towards Chip is possible to read as jealousy. I don't
know that Jennifer and Needy would have gravitated to each
other if they'd met as teens — their bond is old but brittle.
In their final fight, it's the act of Needy ripping off Jennifer's
BFF necklace that cements her end. Jennifer suddenly goes
limp and effectively lets herself be stabbed through the heart
now that her tie to Needy has been symbolically broken. It's
heavy imagery, with their relationship a matter of literal life
and death.

It was important to Kusama that *Jennifer's Body* didn't
sanitize the teen experience or the experience of being a
young woman. Needy and Jennifer didn't have to be perfect exemplars of how young women "should" behave. They

41

needed to feel like real, lived-in characters, and their flaws and imperfections weren't to be glossed over.

"I just feel like it's so important, not just in my own work but in the world, to make more room for the feminine. And I think that that can express itself in this myriad of ways," Kusama told me. "To me, it is as much about a woman standing at a nighttime refrigerator and gorging on a whole chicken and then throwing up a bunch of black sludge as it is to be in a horrible magenta prom dress running through a forest barefoot, trying to save your best friend and the boy you love," she said.

This is something far deeper than celebration or even a pushback against sexist tropes, it's a deeper engagement with how we view gender in ourselves and how we relate to it around us. Kusama continued, "How do we find room for ourselves and for that strain of ourselves — in men *and* women? Because I think it's the thing that [we all] are lacking the most, is this healthy relationship to the feminine, to femaleness and to how that can exist on a spectrum within all of us, and it doesn't have to be something we deny or repress or oppress or defile."

The choice of Megan Fox to play Jennifer feels particularly inspired when hearing Kusama speak. A staple of "lad mags" in the aughts, Fox was on fire, getting tons of media attention and landing major roles. She went straight to shooting *Jonah Hex* after *Jennifer's Body*. While *Jonah Hex* tanked even harder than *Jennifer's Body* just a year later, it was a big-ticket credit, a DC comic book adaptation from a major studio with a giant budget. And Fox was appearing on the covers of major

magazines
Maxim, and
same thing,
was being cov
height of her
from her age ar

There was t
had an objectifyii
a tasteless, drive-
ill-fated interview
Michael Bay was e
peppered with leeri
better actor matter if
you realize you were
self-satisfied asides like
one of the hottest wome
2009 *Esquire* profile incl
tions of Fox's appearance,
eral cleavage" and the visik

When Fox's talent or
it was often with a sense of
implication, sometimes stat
forthright and intelligent thar
hit would suggest," wrote *Th*
referring to the second *Transf*
his review of *Jennifer's Body*, poi
as "an encouraging discovery."[4]
flated with their characters, typec

used to them as
Transformers cha
rough around th
she's the best m
dent, owning h
dressed, and sh
her character's
symbol status
person and as
Fox's tale
characters wi
cially satisfyii
tation with
of vulnerabi
Jennifer's bi
cure. "You
awkwardly
she blew i
and come
entire bar
one coul
anything
"I've
lamb. A
they pu
Lynn F
Jennife
the sac

sit down to talk to men's magazines, there's a certain character that I play."[5]

That Fox is bold and outspoken, a little crass and offensive at times. She doesn't censor herself or feel the need to play nice — or so the popular narrative went. But nothing about her or the way she presented herself points to the stupidity or lack of talent assumed by her surprised interviewers. Nor did she seem to genuinely fit the mold either projected onto her or adopted willingly.

This sounds an awful lot like Jennifer, who sees the Devil's Kettle tragedy for what it is. After the dive bar Melody Lane burns down during the Low Shoulder show, the town comes together, unified by collective mourning. Later deaths, murders committed by the demonic appetite in Jennifer, are similarly commemorated, with vigils and shrines to the deceased. Jennifer doesn't join in though.

With more than a dash of cynicism, she rejects the town's public grieving. On the one hand it's callous: "It already won," Jennifer responds with characteristic snark to biology teacher Mr. Wroblewski's "We can't let that damn fire win." On the other hand, it's an authentic response from someone whose own victimization at Melody Lane isn't given any room or recognition. The PR spin on the tragedy elevates her attackers to heroes, when they are actually profiting off their crimes — which include sacrificing Jennifer and also more than likely setting the fire themselves. When she says, "I tell it like it is" to Needy, justifying her "life is too short to be moping around about some white-trash pig roast," Jennifer cuts through the bullshit of performative mourning. Megan Fox herself never displayed this kind of cruelty or indifference in her public comments, but there's a similarly "unladylike" image (emphasis on the quotation marks) that comes with the way Fox and Jennifer both refused to mince words in favor of telling it like it is.

Outside gender specifically, the weight of all of this everyday drama, as well as the violent and not-so-everyday tragedies, are brought home by a few moments when we zoom out from the teen experience to see the broader world that these kids live in. We have the sacrifice sequence, with its sobering lack of dark comedy, and the very end of the scene when Needy kills Jennifer, when Jennifer's mother walks in and sees what has happened to her daughter.

The fight between Jennifer and Needy itself is punctuated by funny wordplay and absurdity. "My tit," Jennifer says when Needy finally stabs her in the chest. "No, your heart," Needy responds. That final joke reinforces the film's anarchic sense of 2000s cynicism, where even death is something we can hold at arm's length and laugh about. It also serves as a throwback to Jennifer's first on-screen kill, when she puts her victim Jonas's hand on her chest, telling the football jock to feel her broken heart before she kills him. Jennifer conflates tits and hearts first to fake sincerity, then to keep from showing her true heartbreak.

All of that playfully dark banter comes to a screeching halt when Jennifer's mom turns on the light and sees her daughter lying dead in her bedroom. Teenagers often exist in their own worlds, or at least it feels that way. The interpersonal drama of high school and the family home are two entirely different realities, and Jennifer's mother is a reminder of the reality that Jennifer is a teenager, a daughter, and a human being, whatever else she may be. Her life has just ended, and the weight of that lands so much harder when a parent enters the picture.

An earlier cut of *Jennifer's Body* expanded on this by including the funerals of Jennifer's victims, reminding us that, despite the cool detachment with which their deaths are handled, the children — because they really are still kids — meant something to someone, and their murders are tragedies. "Everybody kind of had this moment of adult, parental sorrow that wasn't meant to be funny," Kusama told me, and that left audiences uncomfortable during test screenings. "When we got to the post phase, that kind of tonal schizophrenia was really frightening for people."

An unrated and extended cut of the film expands one of these funerals, complete with the grief of indie/goth kid Colin Gray's parents and friends. We also see Jonas Kozelle's parents mourning, his father flying into a rage and his mother going nearly catatonic. Kusama says that this version is closer to her original intent, and the funeral scene in particular does add a considerable punch to the film.

Of course there's also the more innocent and nostalgic sides of adolescence, like getting excited about a school dance, sneaking drinks at a bar (if you can get away with it), and first love. Needy's mom curls her hair before they take an uncomfortable photo together, her mom standing where Chip should be, smiling enthusiastically while Needy grits her teeth. These moments represent the very best of teen horror, when we get a sense that these kids lead three-dimensional lives.

And the deteriorating relationship between Jennifer and Needy is offset, to some degree, by Needy's oddly normal relationship with Chip. Needy and Chip are a cute couple, and their relationship is, on the whole, a healthy one. Chip is the "nice guy" — his name is Chip Dove for crying out loud — devolving only infrequently into eye rolling jealousy and mansplainy asides (like when he's disappointed that Needy doesn't know how "seminal" Phil Collins is). He's a charming, cute goofball, overall — during his sex scene with Needy, Chip comically mistakes her cries when she has a vision of one of Jennifer's kills for evidence that he's "too big," and he unconvincingly resists his mom's attempts to arm him with pepper spray on the grounds that he's tough enough as it is from using his obviously neglected Bowflex.

Jennifer's Body doesn't glorify virginity like most teen movies, where boys are out for conquest and girls put their bodies and their reputations on the line. In contrast, Needy and Chip's sex life feels low stakes. And it's one of the most believable and tender instances of teen sexuality I've seen in film or television.

"I think it's one of the best, most candid depictions in a mainstream film, of adolescent sex," Colin Geddes told me, while explaining why he chose *Jennifer's Body* for the Midnight Madness lineup. "It's probably my favorite scene in the movie, to be honest," Diablo Cody said at TIFF. "I wanted it to seem very realistic and candid, because we have all of these clichés about movie sex, and it's always very graceful, and organic in a very romantic way, and I liked that in this movie, the kids had to plan to have sex." At the premiere screening Q&A, she also joked about the logistics of sex and how important it was to capture the particular awkwardness of teen sex. "I just feel like I never saw somebody say, 'Put it in' during a sex scene," she explained. "Whereas I think during a regular sexual encounter, I think a time comes where you actually need to deal with the anatomical reality of that — someone's gotta put it in — but in the movies, it always just magically glides into the vagina, so I was like 'Someone needs to go, "Put it in,"' and that happens in this movie, and I feel like if I've made any contribution to cinema at all, that's it."

For Kusama, this sexual relationship also tied into the horror genre and expectations around teen female sexuality: "Needy has this very positive relationship with Chip that's open and awkward, but very real and connected and engaged, and I just felt that instead of what I think has become the cliché of the genre, where somehow a lot of meaningless sex — whatever 'meaningless' really means — leads to murder . . . this was reversing a lot of those tropes."[6]

It's not fair to treat the Needy/Chip and Jennifer/Needy pairings as categorically distinct though. "Friendship" doesn't entirely cut it when describing Jennifer and Needy, whose relationship also leans strongly in romantic directions. The two have a history of playing "boyfriend-girlfriend" together. And their bond is a long-lasting one — "Sandbox love never dies," says Needy in voiceover, with shots of the two playing as young kids.

The overhyped and frequently misunderstood kiss between Jennifer and Needy is the clearest example of their romantic affection for one another. "We always share your bed when we have slumber parties," says Jennifer, talking her way into Needy's arms. If the two girls' friendship seems toxic at times, there's also a great deal of genuine affection between them that suddenly reads differently once they lock lips. In a nice wink to the audience, Jennifer says, "I go both ways" to Needy near the end of the film, when the two are in mortal combat, in response to Needy's "I thought you only murdered boys."

Not that the queer bond between Jennifer and Needy is all that subtextual before the kiss. Hannah Ewens pointed out in *VICE* that Needy's crush on Jennifer is on obvious display when we first see the two at school together, as Needy watches Jennifer's cheerleading routine to the Black Kids' "I'm Not Gonna Teach Your Boyfriend How to Dance with You." The lyrics "You are the girl that I've been dreaming of ever since I was a little girl" especially stick out.[7] Cue the nearby classmate calling Needy and Jennifer "lesbigay." While Chip is also performing, playing the drum for the audience (and his girlfriend), Needy barely notices him. The entire scene revolves around Needy and Jennifer, with shots cutting back and forth between the two, as they excitedly make eye contact and smile and wave to each other.

In another suggestive moment, Needy and Chip's sex scene is intercut with scenes of Jennifer luring and killing

Colin Gray. As Jennifer works herself into a frenzy with some clear sexual overtones, Needy and Chip have a more subdued sexual encounter, but the cutting back and forth between both scenes blurs the events, creating a visual and thematic parallel and connecting Needy to Jennifer, sexually. As the scene goes on, that connection is made literal when Needy starts hallucinating blood and sees Jennifer in her room with her earlier victim Jonas. That connection comes up again when Needy, at the dance, feels Jennifer kissing Chip, his death imminent.

"I read those scenes as inherently difficult, complicated, erotic, charged, and they actually helped, to me, bring a kind of emotional honesty to this fucked-up relationship that we're watching," Kusama explained to me. "When we see toxic friendships, particularly as they are comically portrayed in film and TV, it's easy to have our rational brain say, 'Well yeah, but why? Why would you keep hanging out with somebody who keeps insulting you and leaving you in the dust?' But that scene, in which we realize that they are sometime lovers, solidified so much of what was real about the relationship to me, which is that when you're 17, 18 years old and you're in a combative, problematic relationship with somebody, and you occasionally have intimacy that goes beyond a great conversation at a diner, that is so intense. For regular adults, that's so intense. It's hard to separate the power of these physical and sexual and romantic encounters that create moments of clarifying and understanding your desire, of creating uncomfortable longing."

Hollywood has a sketchy history with its treatment of queerness, especially in horror. Monsters have traditionally been coded as queer, with horror films reflecting the times with references to threats to the nuclear family, homophobic fears of pedophilia, the AIDS crisis, and more. As film scholar Harry M. Benshoff puts it, "To create a broad analogy, monster is to 'normality' as homosexual is to heterosexual."[8]

Jennifer's Body could have easily devolved into a similarly anti-queer vision of monstrosity, with Jennifer's perceived seduction of Needy played as a manipulative ploy. Instead, it's something far more human. In that scene, we see Jennifer trying to maintain the most important relationship in her life, even as she refuses to give up her power or need to kill. And in Needy, we see a desperate belief in the possibility that the Jennifer she knows and loves is still in there. Jennifer initiates the kiss, but Needy is immediately all in, clinging to Jennifer as an active participant before she pulls away, jolted back to the violence the demon in Jennifer has committed.

If you buy into the kiss as bait for straight boys in marketing materials and reviews, you miss something profoundly and tragically beautiful about teen love and queer identity. Jennifer and Needy have hidden this dimension of their relationship, but they've also found validation and connection in each other in a way that feels safe and exclusively theirs. "I don't really remember what happened after that," Jennifer tells Needy about how she survived the attack by Low Shoulder. "I just know that I woke up and found my way back to you." Even overwhelmed by hungry demon animal instinct, she knows to go to Needy. While there, she also suggestively presses her body up against Needy's, sniffing at her, touching her almost sensually, and pressing her mouth to Needy's neck. Her instincts may be predatory, but they're also undeniably sexual. And importantly, the human part of Jennifer, who loves Needy, knows to hold back, refusing to harm her even at her hungriest and most feral.

Kusama was no doubt the right choice of director to frame the kiss scene, and other romantic moments between Needy and Jennifer, in a non-exploitative way, favoring characterization, context, and emotional impact over cheap objectification and unprompted lust or affection. While a non-queer filmmaker could have potentially pulled it off, Kusama was keenly aware of the high stakes of a scene like this, what it would mean to the film as a whole and what depicting it truthfully would look like. A lot has been made, rightfully, of the fact that *Jennifer's Body* was written and directed by women, but it's also important to celebrate it as an iconic queer film.

"I do often refer to myself as queer," Kusama told me. "I've never wanted my ability to love and be loved to be labeled, and so, for me, I've had relationships with women, I've had relationships with men, and now I've found the man that I have a child with and a family with, and all of that is great, but I'm also somebody who is pretty proudly uninterested in wearing heterosexuality as a badge." In a follow-up email, Kusama elaborated: "I have always loved the word 'queer': beyond its meanings associated with sexual preference, to me it implies an emotional expansiveness, a deep imaginative capacity, and a rejection of societal definitions. When I think of myself as queer I like to think about all of the possibilities my humanity might entail."

Fox had recently come out herself, discussing her own bisexuality in the lead-up to *Jennifer's Body*. "I'm not a lesbian," she told *GQ*, almost exactly a year before heading to the TIFF premiere. "I just think that all humans are born with the ability to be attracted to both sexes."⁹ In June 2009, she was more definitive about her own sexuality in an interview with *Esquire*: "I think people are born bisexual and then make subconscious choices based on the pressures of society," she said. "I have no question in my mind about being bisexual."¹⁰

During a Q&A at a ten-year anniversary screening of *Jennifer's Body* at LA's Fantastic Fest, Fox said the film provided her proudest role and was a career favorite, alongside her recurring role on the series *New Girl*.¹¹ Both Jennifer and *New Girl*'s Reagan Lucas are, coincidentally or not, the only times Fox has played explicitly queer characters, to my knowledge.

The erasure of Jennifer's and Needy's queerness upon the film's initial release was likely of little surprise to bisexual people. It's a process I still see and experience constantly today. There's a common joke that to be bisexual is to be in a perpetual state of coming out as bisexual — no matter how many times we say it, something just doesn't seem to stick. Megan Fox's bisexuality is no exception: it has never received much recognition nor respect in the press; you're more likely to find Fox in "Stars you didn't know were queer" clickbait listicles than to see her acknowledged as any kind of queer icon. Her bisexuality has been effectively written off as part of her perceived wild child persona, which was particularly noxious in the lead-up to a film like *Jennifer's Body*. "Megan Fox *admits* to being bisexual," said *Esquire* (emphasis added).[12] *GQ* discussed Fox's "confessions," focusing on a "reckless" first year in Hollywood that included getting tattoos and developing a flirtation with a woman who danced at a local strip club.[13] This is the sensationalizing and stigmatizing language of shocking exposés of "deviant" behavior, rather than reporting on reality: a young woman gets moderately inked and explores her sexuality. This kind of coverage of Fox's sexuality is a natural extension of the reviews that could only understand the kiss between Needy and Jennifer as performed for the straight male gaze.

Jennifer's Body wasn't just exploring the teen experience but more specifically the queer teen experience, and providing representation that went all but unnoticed — to put it generously — in popular reviews of the film, despite the queer women in front of and behind the camera, and despite some very explicit nods even beyond the kiss. In the final fight between Jennifer and Needy, when Needy attacks with a box cutter, Jennifer quips, "Do you buy all your murder weapons at Home Depot? God, you're butch." With one line, Jennifer ties Needy to lesbian identities while acknowledging the shifting gender roles in their relationship. They used to play "boyfriend-girlfriend," which is a heteronormative way to frame their queer love, but it also points to how power plays out between them in gendered terms. We can surmise that Jennifer is used to playing the more dominant role of the boyfriend, but as Needy takes control, that dynamic shifts. It's also a clever play on the Final Girl trope. If the Final Girl is meant to be more boyish or masculine than other girls, calling Needy "butch" in her most Final Girl moment resituates this gender-bending of horror heroines into the realm of the distinctly non-male world of lesbian communities.

And capping off the film's solid play on queer coming of age is its indie/emo soundtrack. One of the film's first shots gives us a clear view of the wall of band posters in Jennifer's bedroom. Front and center is a Fall Out Boy pinup, signaling her emo interests. Later we see Chip's walls, adorned with Motion City Soundtrack and Four Year Strong posters. The film's soundtrack features songs by groups such as Silversun Pickups, Cute Is What We Aim For, Dashboard Confessional, Panic! at the Disco, music that, as Hannah Ewens points out, was part of the overtly bisexual Myspace emo scene and reinforces the queer narrative beats throughout.[14]

Teen music culture more generally is central to the film and gets its strongest representation in Low Shoulder and their recurring hit song "Through the Trees," which becomes an anthem for the Devil's Kettle bar fire thanks to the band's shameless capitalization on the disaster they (very likely) caused. "Through the Trees" was written for the film by Test Your Reflex (now Wilding) front man Ryan Levine, with Levine providing vocals for Nikolai, who was in turn played by Adam Brody, whose character emulates The Killers' Brandon Flowers. (Lots of layers, but stay with me.) Levine plays the Low Shoulder guitarist on screen, with the rest of Test Your Reflex as the other members of the band.

The song is perfectly evocative of the pop-punk emo ballads that had effectively peaked by 2009. In that way, a band like Low Shoulder would legitimately have needed a miracle — or, you know, the assistance of Satan — to break out and make their mark in a world that already had My Chemical Romance, The Killers, Fall Out Boy, and so many more established bands for teens to listen to. And they know it better than anyone. "Do you know how hard it is to make it as an indie band these days? There's so many of us, and we're all so cute, and it's like, if you don't get on *Letterman* or some retarded soundtrack, you're screwed, okay? Satan is our only hope," Nikolai tells Jennifer before sacrificing her.

The sacrifice itself is a cleverly grim update on the Faustian legend of blues guitarist Robert Johnson. Johnson is said to have gone to a local crossroads in Clarksdale, Mississippi, in the 1930s, where he sold his soul to the devil in exchange for his considerable musical talent. But why sell your own soul when you could sacrifice a virgin's?

Jennifer's Body pokes fun at the oversaturation of indie rockers in the late 2000s, even while celebrating it with a soundtrack full of catchy songs and posters of bands du jour. The casting of Adam Brody is a well-earned wink to the audience: Brody's breakout role was as music-obsessed Seth Cohen in Fox's teen soap *The O.C.*, a show that represents the peak of TV soundtrack culture, arguably responsible for the massive popularity of Death Cab for Cutie, in a phenomenon dubbed "the Seth effect" by Amy Phillips in 2004.[15]

Nikolai is the cynical, dark mirror image of Seth Cohen's quintessential nice guy. Seth was defined by a sense of authenticity, introducing young viewers to the really good indie stuff that top 40 radio wouldn't give you. That carefully curated character sold a ton of soundtracks — or official *The O.C.* "mixes." Nikolai, on the other hand, is all about playing the nice guy as he games the system, dismissively spewing slurs about the very mechanism of his own potential success — all while producing music that sounds exactly like it belongs on "some retarded soundtrack." Brody's casting on *The O.C.* followed a smaller role as rock band front man Dave in *Gilmore Girls*. Brody's established nice-guy status is subverted in his turn as Nikolai — and again in his roles in later films like *Ready or Not* and especially *Promising Young Woman*. By casting against type here, Cody and Kusama are having their cake and eating it, too, taking full advantage of an existing romanticized vision of the music industry while simultaneously tearing it down and exposing its dark side. It's a dense, rewarding intertextual nod to Seth Cohen and the '00s mechanics of mainstreaming alternative culture.

Low Shoulder literalizes yesteryear's fears that rock and roll is "the Devil's music" made to ensnare our youth. Superficially, it's a hilarious bit. But when we get into what that means for Jennifer and her town, the metaphor takes a sharp turn. Instead of parodying the way reactionary old conservatives fear pop culture, Low Shoulder's crime and subsequent success illuminate the ever-present threat of men in a misogynistic, patriarchal, and capitalist society. We never needed to fear that kids were being brainwashed and recruited into devil-worshipping cults through music. What we needed to fear is the much scarier, run-of-the-mill evil that lurks everywhere.

4

Gods and Monsters

Imagine what the movie posters would have looked like if the studio had recognized the film's greatest asset: not Megan Fox as titillating high school it girl, but Megan Fox as flesh-eating, black-sludge-spewing monster. Because even as a demon-possessed killer, she's a profoundly appealing character, and Megan Fox delivers a pitch-perfect performance. Jennifer is cruel, to be sure, but she is also enviably, unapologetically powerful. "I am a god," she tells Needy when she's first discovering the extent of her newfound abilities, which include immediately healing from injury and, later, hovering.

Not that Jennifer was meek and powerless before she started snacking on boy flesh. She can already confidently buy her own drinks at Melody Lane, despite being underage, for example. "I cannot wait until I'm old enough to get wasted," she tells Needy when they first enter the bar. Similarly, Jennifer owns her sexuality in ways not strictly socially sanctioned, and even problematized within the film. She casually talks about having had anal sex and flirts openly with who she wants, including the very police cadet Roman (played by a pre-fame Chris Pratt) who she lost her "backdoor" virginity to. But Roman knows a line's being crossed. He's an adult, admonishing her for smoking a cigarette even while he inappropriately flirts with her. But when she flirts back and grabs his crotch, he gets embarrassed and tells her not to, "not here," and looks to make sure no one's noticed the exchange with a minor. Jennifer is comfortable playing with power dynamics when engaging with her male admirers, but she's still a young woman in a patriarchy. Moments later, we see her awkwardly flirt with Nikolai, telling him he and his band play their instruments "really good," in a moment that's innocently adorable until it's clear Nikolai is primed to switch into exploitation mode.

Megan Fox's own accounts of portraying Jennifer, and the pleasures of tapping into her character, definitely reinforce a celebratory reading of her behavior: "My character was extremely unapologetic and really irreverent, and that's enjoyable, to have the freedom to do that."[1]

Karyn Kusama saw something similarly appealing in Jennifer: "What I loved about Jennifer was her lack of apology. She was just all id. She was all appetite. She was all about doing things for herself. And that selfishness is actually not a way that we've seen a woman or a girl depicted very frequently. And so, I have to say that's something I celebrated in her. There was this lack of consequence in her mind that was kind of refreshing . . . She's that bull in a china shop, and I loved that she came in this pert, beautiful package that looks like Megan Fox."

There's a very dark side to that, too, obviously, and not just because Jennifer eventually eats people, but also specifically because of who she eats and how. With the exception of Ahmet, who Jennifer eats out of desperation and opportunity, her victims aren't entirely random. Jonas was best friends with Craig, who shows an interest in Jennifer at the bar before the fire. "What up, Craig?" she responds, with all the enthusiasm of someone noticing they have a hangnail. Is Jennifer getting back at the men who sacrificed her, at the boys who relentlessly hit on her through surrogates? She reduces her victims to mere bodies to consume, just as she was objectified and consumed. Colin Gray only meets his fate after asking Jennifer out, despite the two seemingly having nothing in common — does she see him as another shallow boy who objectifies her? Colin isn't guilty in the way that Nikolai is, but he fits a familiar type (the shy and harmless indie kid) who Jennifer has every reason to be wary of by now. In his case, she seems to also make her selection based on Needy's own interest in Colin. Jennifer taking what she wants may be appealing on some level, but there's also still a sense that she's lashing out at the wrong people and intentionally harming Needy, the person she loves most. Jennifer's warped justice doesn't let us off easy as viewers looking for black-and-white morality.

Even before she was boy flesh–powered, Jennifer had a domineering personality. "You and me are going out tonight," Jennifer says to Needy, in her first scene of dialogue. It's certainly a bossy way to speak to a friend, especially one who already had plans that she instantly alters for you. That hierarchical dynamic is reinforced in the next scene, in Needy's narration after Jennifer tells her to "wear something cute" to the show: "'Wear something cute' meant something very specific in Jennifer Speak," says Needy. "It meant I couldn't look like a total zero but couldn't upstage her either. I could expose my stomach but never my cleavage. Tits were her trademark." Jennifer, a young woman likely to be underestimated, wields control and power where she can — a kind of mundane monstrosity that is part survival mechanism and part damaging toxic personality trait.

"I have outrageous friends who sometimes might take a lot of air out of the room, but I give them that space because I kind of love them, or I worship them, or I want to be them in some way, but in the end it comes with a price, and so that's really what the story is meant to be exploring," Kusama told me. "In some respects, we recognize something true about Jennifer, which is that she's like this funny, obnoxious, confident, beautiful teenage girl, but she has a quality of monstrous cruelty and lack of empathy that just gets magnified in some respects once she's lost her humanity."

The seeming contradictions in Jennifer make her relatable, to some degree. She looks for acceptance. She takes what she wants. She's unapologetic. She's critical of herself.

She's judgmental. She lashes out. She's caring. She's funny and sarcastic. She's smart. She's oblivious.

When Needy says that "Jennifer's evil," she's right, but Jennifer is also her friend and sometime lover. She's the villain of the film, to a degree, set against Needy as hero. The film may be named for Jennifer, and 20th Century Fox certainly marketed around Megan Fox, but it's Needy's story. It's told from her perspective, and it primarily follows her storyline.

"It's very interesting to me that we keep looking at Jennifer as the protagonist of the story, because — and this happened at every level, this happened in how we discussed the costumes and the story beats with our actors, and the marketing with the marketing team — it's like everybody forgot that Jennifer isn't the main character. Needy Lesnicki is," Kusama told me. "It's like we can't help but offer that primary role, in a funny way, to this monstrous character, when in fact, the story is so much about what it means to be on the receiving end of that behavior. What it means to be like most regular people, which is making a lot of room for the noisiest person in the room."

There absolutely is something appealing about the noisiest person in the room, which is why we make that extra space for people who don't always deserve it. Kusama, Cody, Fox, and Seyfried all work together to establish Jennifer as someone appealing in exactly this way, as someone with agency and self-assurance that's actually quite enviable. The vast majority of us are Needys. We can see ourselves in the way she lets Jennifer steer their social lives, and we can relate to her awe and affection at this powerful force of nature dominating our screens.

Jennifer's transformation into a literal horror-movie monster is worth dwelling on. The impression that she takes control of her body after it has been violated feels just, but it also comes at the cost of possession and further, ongoing violation, all while her male attackers walk away free and benefit from their crime, at least for a time. Her initial trauma is echoed when she has to feed on human flesh, an impulse that isn't Jennifer's but that of the demon who holds her hostage. Jennifer only gets brief reprieves, a few weeks of happiness at a time, before the horror of what happened to her comes back, forcefully and physically. The hellish realities of PTSD in this case are rather appropriately literally *from hell*. That assault is, in a lot of ways, the lynchpin of the film. The moment that explains just about everything Cody and Kusama are up to.

"It's very interesting to me that when we would test the film and when I would talk about the movie with executives, they would always describe that scene as 'the gang rape,' instead of as the sacrifice," Kusama told me. And it does play as a rape scene in a lot of ways. The ritual scene itself is devoid of any sexual violence, but the event is definitely coded as rape — Jennifer explicitly asks the musicians if they're rapists as their intentions slowly become clearer to her, and Needy grimly describes the make of their van as "an '89 Rapist" on the phone with Chip. They're not rapists, as far as we know, and yet the sight of a teen girl driven out to the forest at night by gleefully misogynist men who laugh and joke over her sobbing and pleas for freedom is absolutely chilling in a familiar way.

That Cody, Kusama, and the film's cast were able to achieve the right tone here, fitting perfectly well into the film without undercutting itself through any of the kind of ironic self-awareness that permeates so much of the movie is a testament to how precisely calibrated *Jennifer's Body* is and how intentionally it delivers its thematic punch.

The sacrifice strips Jennifer of her agency (temporarily) and her humanity (permanently). When Nikolai pauses to ask, "What's your name again? Tiffany?" Jennifer responds forcefully and tragically, "My name is Jennifer," asserting her personhood in a futile attempt to reach whatever empathy these men might possess. It's a haunting and frankly difficult scene to watch — viscerally difficult. It needs to be. It still takes my breath away every time I see it, countless viewings later.

"I think I felt really deeply that I had to protect the reality of what we were depicting, which is the theft of someone's dignity and humanity," Kusama explained to me. "To me, in the most uncomfortable way, it exists as a sort of mission statement for the film." She elaborated on the process of filming the scene, and how sobering it was not only within the film but on set too: "I found it so challenging to have to see Megan suffering like that. And her suffering was real, her terror was real. She was extremely upset after we shot the scene, and no wonder. It's so horrifying. And I look now at that scene, and what really fascinates me is that it mirrors stories I heard of what the horror of sexual assault actually is, which is this complete inability to see a person."

The dehumanization and exploitation of Jennifer finds dark parallels in Fox's own career and public image, a woman sacrificed for profit and prestige. "In talking about all of this more recently . . . I realized that in filming that scene where they sacrifice me, that was really reflective of, I felt, my relationship with movie studios at that point, because I felt that that was what they were willing to do, to literally bleed me dry," Fox told Cody during their tenth anniversary sit-down. "They didn't care about my health, my well-being, mentally, emotionally, at all. And they were willing to sacrifice me physically as long as they got what they wanted out of it. And it didn't matter how many times I spoke up and said, 'I'm hurting. This isn't right. I need someone to protect me. This is going on. Someone needs to listen.' It didn't matter at all."[2]

She explained in an interview with *Billboard* that the moment the band laughs at Jennifer made the scene particularly hard to shoot. "There was something very intense, something that triggered me when they would get to that part of the scene," she said. "Being mocked in such an excruciatingly flippant way pulled that performance out of me. I wasn't acting. Just reacting to being devalued."[3] Fox is underselling her skill in a scene where she shows amazing range and deep empathy for her character. No doubt she was tapping into her own experiences, as she said, and in allowing herself that vulnerability, she turned in a haunting performance.

This is the moment when our suspicions about Low Shoulder are finally confirmed, when Needy's demonology research pays off. It's the moment we get, quite late in the film, the full context of Jennifer's transformation and those guilty of doing this to her. The strength and agency she exhibited is suddenly taken from her. "We don't need to talk if you don't want to," Nikolai says to her when she asks where they're taking her. It's a brilliantly simple way to establish his power in the moment. The dynamic is dialed up as the band continues to sing over Jennifer's screams while Nikolai stabs her, again and again. Jennifer the person truly is reduced to Jennifer's body in this moment, stripped of her voice even in what are meant to be her final moments.

If we read the scene as a metaphor for Fox herself, it also points to the broader, systemic failings of the industry, which allows for people (often women) to be exploited for the gains of others. Fox's outspokenness landed her in hot water more than once, including calling out Disney for making one of its stars, then-18-year-old Vanessa Hudgens, apologize when a nude photo, taken privately, was leaked to the press. "You shouldn't have to apologize," she said of the incident. "Someone betrayed Vanessa, but no one's angry at that person. *She* had to apologize. I hate Disney for making her do that. Fuck Disney."[4]

Fox had her own run-ins with leaked nudes and the bizarre cottage industry of celebrity gossip blogs, arguably at its peak at the end of the aughts. She has said she had to beg a *Jennifer's Body* producer to intervene to keep paparazzi photos of her swimming nude on a closed set (Jennifer was rinsing off after her first on-screen kill) from appearing on gossip king Perez

Hilton's then bafflingly popular blog.[5] The whole ordeal is a shameful example of the kinds of invasive violations that were part and parcel of Hilton's brand of entertainment media, which persist in different forms to this day, all in the name of clickbait celebrity access. While stars like Megan Fox and Vanessa Hudgens should have been protected by the studios making bank off of their talents, they were left to fend for themselves and shamed and blamed if something went awry.

Diablo Cody has praised Fox for how she presented herself back then. "I could read Megan Fox interviews from 2009 all day because I love that she was speaking her mind. But she was punished for it," Cody told *The Playlist* in 2018.[6] A year later, she told *New York* that "the world should have been thanking Megan Fox for those incredible, candid, real-ass interviews she was giving at the time. That girl's balls . . ."[7]

These supposed outbursts were generally treated as the tantrums of an ungrateful star who'd had fame handed to her. Fox's success was frequently misattributed to Michael Bay and his *Transformers* franchise. The myth of overnight success comes up a lot in profiles of Fox. Yes, *Transformers* was absolutely a defining moment in Fox's career, a turning point in making her a global superstar. But it came out in 2007, and Fox's first credited role was in 2001 in the Olsen Twins' *Holiday in the Sun*. She spent the next six years working consistently in film and TV, with highlights including a guest role in the hit sitcom *Two and a Half Men* and a major part in the feature film *Confessions of a Teenage Drama Queen* in 2004, as well as a regular role in two seasons of ABC's *Hope & Faith* from

2004 to 2006. As a child actor who hustled and paid her dues in the industry for half a decade, it's more than a little unfair to pretend Fox was plucked from obscurity and dropped into the role of a lifetime.

That narrative of ingratitude reached its zenith when Fox bit the hand that supposedly fed her in an interview with *Wonderland*. During an infamous Q&A, Fox called out Bay's unprofessional behavior on his film sets, including endangering cast and crew and engaging in casual sexism towards his star — "Just be sexy," she quoted him as saying in response to her requests for direction.[8] None of Fox's rather concerning criticisms of the director seemed to send up any red flags in the industry, but when she called him a tyrant and invoked Hitler, it was open season on the young actress.

On September 11, 2009, effectively the same day as *Jennifer's Body* had its midnight world premiere at TIFF, three of Michael Bay's crew members wrote an open letter to Megan Fox.[9] The anonymous authors of the letter addressed their screed to "all Michael Bay fans," and it was truly vile, from focusing leeringly on Fox's body, to repeating the myth of Bay plucking her from obscurity, to denigrating her acting skills using loaded, sexist language. By the end, they sum it all up with "Megan really is a thankless, classless, graceless, and shall we say unfriendly bitch," and fantasize about her character being crushed to death in the opening scene of the next *Transformers* film.

Bay didn't exactly have his hands clean in this whole letter-writing fiasco. The letter was posted to his own website. It was quickly taken down, and Bay released his own statement, saying in part: "I don't condone the crew letter to Megan. And I don't condone Megan's outlandish quotes."[10] Didn't he condone the crew letter, though? It was on his own website, after all.

This was all unraveling while Megan Fox was in Toronto promoting *Jennifer's Body* and attending its premiere. The film's programmer, Colin Geddes, told me that there was an odd sense of foreboding that hung over the event, like a fear that it might come up or that Fox might say more about Bay. "At the time, everyone, I think, was really nervous," he remembered. "I felt that there was this energy in the room, and it probably was because of that."

In the end, Fox exited the third *Transformers* film during preproduction. How exactly that went down has been a source of debate ever since. Fox says she quit, expecting to be fired eventually anyway,[11] while Bay has suggested that producer Steven Spielberg instructed him to fire her.[12] Meanwhile, Paramount's official statement maintains that the studio chose "at its sole election" not to bring Fox back.[13]

These types of backlashes and controversies have a way of ballooning and really sticking to actors' reputations. "It's weird, because you might think now, 'Oh, that was a minor story,'" Diablo Cody told *Vox* in 2018. "The tone of the coverage of our movie was almost 80 percent about her feud with Michael Bay!"[14]

It's impossible to quantify what a reputation for being "difficult" might have on a career like Fox's — the #MeToo movement certainly showed that it's a label that sticks to actresses in toxic and lasting ways, as when Peter Jackson said he abandoned plans to work with Ashley Judd and Mira Sorvino on his *Lord of the Rings* trilogy based on dubious warnings from the now-disgraced Harvey Weinstein.[15]

"I feel like I was out in front of the #MeToo movement before the #MeToo movement happened," Fox told Diablo Cody in 2019, acknowledging the needle moving towards believing women and pushing back against institutional sexism. "I was speaking out and saying, 'Hey, these things are happening to me, and they're not okay,' and everyone was like, 'Oh, fuck you. We don't care. You deserve it, because of how you talk. Because of how you look. Because of how you dress. Because of the jokes you make.'"[16]

Karyn Kusama, looking back at *Jennifer's Body* ten years later, summed it up perfectly. "The hostility toward Megan," she told *BuzzFeed*, "seemed really to come from sort of a desire to possess and debase her and an inability to effectively do that."[17] And as Diablo Cody has put it, "Megan is specifically being paid to and pressured to be a sexy actress and then is punished for being so."[18]

Megan Fox was certainly punished, no longer landing top-billed roles. She was nominated for worst actress in both *Jennifer's Body* and *Transformers: Revenge of the Fallen* at the Golden Raspberry Awards (Razzies). She later "won" worst supporting actress in 2015 for her role in *Teenage Mutant Ninja Turtles*. But were they responding to the reels or the reputation? Megan Fox is a perfect example of how dubious the Razzies are as a self-professed parodic or satirical anti-awards show, a scornful instead of celebratory antidote to the Oscars. Movies like the *Transformers* series aren't vying for Oscar-level industry recognition, so to lampoon them feels a tad easy. But to dunk on *Jennifer's Body* and Fox in 2009 is to punch down, all in the name of arbitrary, or disturbingly regressive, taste distinction.

Like Fox, Cody hasn't felt like there's been any room for her in the #MeToo or Time's Up movement or in broader conversations about the treatment of women in Hollywood, despite the elevation of *Jennifer's Body* to cult status. "I'm still terrified people will say, 'Well she was a stripper. We don't really care. Does she really have a right to talk about being sexually objectified, or having been put through shit in Hollywood? Because she made that choice for herself, and her story is not valid.' So, I'm scared," Cody told Fox in 2019, using language and rationale almost identical to Fox's.[19] In short, both see victim-blaming as a given if the victim in question isn't deemed pure and likeable enough.

Would Jennifer have been believed? Low Shoulder immediately zeroes in on her as the right kind of victim for the sacrifice. Nikolai says he's known plenty of girls like Jennifer, girls who "love to show it off, but they do not give it up." That's frankly the language of a rapist: "They do not give it up" comes with both the horrific resentment used to justify taking "it" without consent and the placement of fault on the victim.

Kusama's description of the scene and her impressions of it as a stand-in for sexual violence also touched on the political context almost a decade later. When we spoke, she brought up

73

the case of Brett Kavanaugh, who, in 2018, was appointed to the Supreme Court of the United States after a lengthy investigation into allegations that he had sexually assaulted Christine Blasey Ford: "The laughing at Jennifer in her moment of most terror and the degradation of that at this point has been made part of the American lexicon. In a Supreme Court justice's hearing, we hear about how he laughed at the woman who says he assaulted her, or tried to."

Vox's Constance Grady summed up this parallel less than a month after Kavanaugh was sworn in: "Watching [the sacrifice scene] in 2018 brings up unavoidable echoes of Christine Blasey Ford's testimony about Brett Kavanaugh's alleged assault on her when she was a teenager, of the phrase 'Indelible in the hippocampus is the laughter.' Jennifer's pain is funny to these men. For them, it's a lark. But for her, it's a moment of trauma that is going to change her forever."[20]

And it does change her, very literally. Through the assault, she loses ownership of her body to a demon, her humanity just about destroyed. There is a trauma-fueled logic in the gender of her victims: boys who can roughly stand in for those who made her a victim first.

This all brings *Jennifer's Body* in line with yet another horror tradition: the rape-revenge film. As film scholar Alexandra Heller-Nicholas puts it, "At its most basic level, a rape-revenge film is one whereby a rape that is central to the narrative is punished by an act of vengeance, either by the victim themselves or by an agent (a lawyer, policeman, or, most commonly, a loved one or family member)."[21] If we make room for figurative rape, which Heller-Nicholas does in her discussions of films like Quentin Tarantino's *Kill Bill* and *Death Proof*, then it's worth considering that Jennifer chooses her victims to enact figurative revenge, before Needy can directly avenge her by killing Low Shoulder at the film's end. The most famous, or infamous, rape-revenge heroine is also coincidentally named Jennifer. *I Spit on Your Grave*'s Jennifer Hills goes about killing the country hicks who gang-raped her, methodically taking them out one by one in cathartically gruesome ways, including castrating the group's ringleader and letting him bleed to death.

Horror monsters are often freeing in this way. We're invited to identify with them or with what they stand for even as we see their flaws and the threats they pose. Rape-revenge may be the subgenre with the greatest claim to the sympathetic "monster." A society that allows women to be abused in this way, with little recourse to official channels of justice, is primed for the rape-revenge film, which offers one of the most righteous agents of vigilante justice imaginable.

"Few horror films have totally unsympathetic Monsters," though, argues horror film scholar Robin Wood. "In many (notably the *Frankenstein* films) the Monster is clearly the emotional center, and much more human than the cardboard representatives of normality."[22] Wood's premise in his now seminal 1978 essay "Return of the Repressed" is that horror films, by and large, offer us a seductive tension between normality and its opposite, that the monster is a threat to what is deemed normal in an ostensibly healthy society.

But it's not healthy, it's just normative, writes Wood. "I use 'normality' here in a strictly non-evaluative sense to mean simply 'conformity to the dominant social norms'; one must firmly resist the common tendency to treat the word as if it were more or less synonymous with 'health.'" Those dominant social norms are hardly neutral or natural. Normality tends to be depicted via heterosexual pairings, the family unit, respect for traditional forms of authority, and the like.[23]

Horror films smash that normality. Cops are bumbling idiots. Politicians are corrupt. The military is psychotic. Parents pose a mortal threat. Consumerism is death.

Horror can often be conservative or reactionary in its politics, with the status quo conspicuously upheld when it's challenged by monsters. "Monsters are threats to cultural order and they must be destroyed through extreme means," write Ernest Mathijs and Jamie Sexton in *Cult Cinema: An Introduction*. "Cult horror films, however, add subversions, ambiguities, and contradictions so that it becomes unclear whether or not restoration of the order is a good thing, or the ends justify the means, or the film itself is actually siding with its story."[24] They later add: "Visit any horror fan convention or festival and invariably the monsters achieve most of the attention and praise."[25] Jennifer isn't the protagonist of *Jennifer's Body*; even as the titular character, we're cued to her loss of subjectivity in the way the title focuses not on her humanity but specifically on her body. But she's the character most often celebrated because she's exactly the kind of cult monster Mathijs and Sexton are talking about. Simply destroying her means burying what was done to her without addressing the root problem. It means accepting the status quo, to some extent, and restoring the "order" that would let bands like Low Shoulder prey on their young female fans and get away with it. That bleak conclusion is avoided, to a degree, when Needy becomes a monster herself, taking the life not only of her best friend but also of the men who harmed and transformed her. Needy is "infected" by Jennifer in their final battle, continuing the cycle of violence initiated by Low Shoulder, but there is a cathartic sense that she's setting things right by film's end, even if it comes at the great cost of shouldering Jennifer's curse.

The righteous rage soundtrack for Needy's revenge, by the way, is "Violet" by Hole, the band whose song "Jennifer's Body" inspired the title of the film. That 1994 track is about a woman who is abducted, murdered, and dismembered, literalizing the cultural objectification of women as physical violence. It's hard not to also draw a few connections between the film and its namesake song, sung by Courtney Love, a woman who faced her own backlashes by music fans eager to treat her as an obnoxious footnote in the story of her late husband, Kurt Cobain. There's a special satisfaction in seeing Needy kill the members of Low Shoulder, not just avenging Jennifer but doing so to the angry vocals of a woman so unjustly scorned within the world of rock and roll.

It's perhaps not surprising that on the holiday for all things monstrous, Jennifer is a popular costume choice. "I have in recent years noticed a lot of Jennifer Checks out at Halloween," said Megan Fox, during a tenth anniversary Q&A with Karyn

Kusama.[26] A quick Twitter or Google search brings up tons of such costumes on Halloween and at horror conventions, along with fan art, with Jennifer taking up a lot of room in fans' hearts. Variations on the statement "Megan Fox in *Jennifer's Body* made me gay" are a staple of the fandom, and it's hyperbolic but not generally ironic in tone. The statement obviously plays on Fox's good looks, but it's also a genuine acknowledgment that Jennifer, for all of her monstrosity and victimhood, is also liberated and liberating. She's appealing in the way she makes the most of what happened to her, embracing her powers and leaning into her romantic love for Needy. The line between Jennifer the enviable queer alpha teen and the murderous demon possessing her isn't always clear, but there's certainly a sense that Jennifer is still allowed to be herself and that some of her behavior is just a bolder version of who she always was.

When Jennifer says "I tell it like it is" to Needy, it's a line that's insufferable and enviable at the same time. She's defiant in a way that's denied to women, and queer women specifically, after all. We all long to say and do whatever we want, knowing full well that polite society needs us to show *some* restraint. But some social norms are genuinely oppressive, and testing those limits is part of creating a healthy society. Calling out the inequities of which rules apply to whom is one way to effect change and break down barriers.

Cult audiences know the value of breaking rules all too well. Yelling at the screen and throwing things isn't a normal part of going to the movies, but it's become a ritualized part of screenings of films like *The Rocky Horror Picture Show* and *The Room*. Society hasn't fallen into chaos just because some cinemagoers have challenged what it means to take part in a public screening, just like society hasn't fallen into chaos as various marginalized people claim space that we were always entitled to.

The injustices faced by Jennifer have been a major part of the film's resurgence, and undoubtedly of its cult bona fides. Her attack comes up in virtually every reappraisal, framing Jennifer as, if not an outright hero, definitely an antihero who we root for.

"You're killing people," Needy says to Jennifer, once she's caught on to what's going on. "No," says Jennifer, as though it's the most obvious truth imaginable, "I'm killing *boys*." The line feels custom-made to elicit a cheer from a midnight movie crowd that wants to identify with a monster who is overcorrecting social ills. It's easy to get behind within the logic of cult cinema. And within the logic of a cultural reckoning. A cultural reckoning with systemic abuse, with queer erasure, with social inequities, and more.

"*Jennifer's Body* made me gay" is a cheeky way to say the film gives us certain necessary permissions. A patriarchal, heteronormative society (and patriarchal, heteronormative entertainment) stifles certain identities, certain ways of existing in the world. Jennifer, in all her unrestrained agency, offers a different path. She reverses the power dynamics that have been forced on her — "No, I'm killing *boys*" — and represents the privilege of living without limits and without conscience, at least for a time.

This all goes a long way to explaining why Jennifer is so appealing. It's no accident that she's the hottest and coolest girl in school. It's no accident that she's queer and sexually liberated. And it's no accident that her monstrosity is consistently linked to her gender and sexuality either. As feminist horror scholar Barbara Creed would call her, Jennifer is the "monstrous-feminine."

"The reasons why the monstrous-feminine horrifies her audience are quite different from the reasons why the male monster horrifies his audience," argues Creed. "As with all other stereotypes of the feminine, from virgin to whore, she is defined in terms of her sexuality. The phrase 'monstrous-feminine' emphasizes the importance of gender in the construction of her monstrosity."[27]

Jennifer's monstrosity is absolutely tied to femininity and sexuality. In the eyes of Low Shoulder, she's both virgin and whore. In her supernatural form, she's a succubus, a man-eater, and a possessed woman. In her human form, she's seen by her classmates as a string of stereotypes: prom queen, slut, bitch.

"I think there's nothing scarier than a bitch," said Cody of Jennifer at the Toronto International Film Festival. "I think the bitch should just take her place in the catalog of classic horror characters: like Dracula, Frankenstein, and a bitchy, attractive woman."[28] The bitch-as-Hollywood-monster can't function without a society that defines appropriate roles for women, though, and Cody and Kusama don't let us off the hook if we choose to blame Jennifer for her perceived bitchiness — we see that it's a valuable tool for her in a world full of Low Shoulders.

Jennifer's monstrosity may be frightening, but it is, perhaps surprisingly, also seductive. That contradiction is at the heart of a lot of classic horror: fear and lust have been happy bedmates since the very early days of the genre. In *The Cabinet of Dr. Caligari*, the sleepwalker Cesare sneaks into a woman's room at night to lustfully abduct her. In 1942's *Cat People*, a woman turns into a man-eating jaguar when she's aroused by or jealous of her husband. In 1983's *The Hunger*, Susan Sarandon's Sarah Roberts loses herself to the lustfully queer world of vampires played by David Bowie and Catherine Deneuve.

The most obviously well-known instance of a seductive killer, though, is probably Count Dracula. Virtually every version of Bram Stoker's iconic, genre-defining vampire is both menacing and alluring. He represents the outsider, threatening disruption of the status quo, but with that is an appealing sense that Dracula is a symbol of liberation. By turning you into a vampire like him, he promises to give you dominion over your own life (or afterlife), which is almost always depicted through overt sensuality and sexuality in the novel and film adaptations, as well as in later vampire texts like *The Hunger*.

The Rocky Horror Picture Show, referenced directly in *Jennifer's Body*, takes that to its extreme. Dr. Frank-N-Furter, a cross between Dracula and Victor Frankenstein, welcomes painfully boring newlyweds Brad and Janet into his secluded mansion when their car breaks down. The "sweet transvestite from Transexual, Transylvania" opens Brad's and Janet's eyes to exciting — but dangerous — alternatives to their dreams of repressed sexuality and a nuclear family. *Rocky Horror*'s enduring cult appeal, with fans dressing as their favorite countercultural characters while cheering on the queer sexual liberation of Brad and Janet, points to some kind of cultural yearning to escape what is "normal."

Even outside of sex and sex appeal, the very best monsters are always at least a little enticing. Straddling the line between excitement and fear is probably the best way to explain the pleasures of watching horror. Why we're entertained by fear is a topic of conversation and debate that likely won't ever be definitively put to rest, but the fundamental reality that we're having fun even while we're frightened is what horror fandom is built on. That tension can potentially tell us a lot about the nature of our fears and desires.

"Central to the effect and fascination of horror films is their fulfillment of our nightmare wish to smash the norms that oppress us and which our moral conditioning teaches us to revere," writes Wood. Not eating human flesh is probably a little outside the realm of the "norms that oppress us," but it's also not *that* far off. Jennifer is used to being objectified and reduced to a body, to being consumed. Literally feeding on the flesh of boys allows her to flip the script and smash the norms that oppress her, in this case the patriarchy. Wood's theory holds up in *Jennifer's Body*, tying it, and her, to rich traditions of the genre.

Think of zombies here, similarly threatening and emancipatory. Coupled with the fear of being assimilated into a horde of thoughtless consumption machines is the cathartic sight of society being razed to the ground. Every broken, backwards facet of our cultures can be eliminated, and we can start fresh. Plus, zombies see what they want, and they take it. It's why so many zombie movies include a "shopping spree," in which the human survivors have the chance to raid stores for much-needed supplies, usually along with some frivolous luxuries. Even the zombies themselves, craving flesh and taking it, have an agency that we don't. We want what the monsters have, whether that's the freedom to be horrible when we want to be, or the freedom to just be who we are and live without judgment, proudly brainy, slutty, goth, queer, or whatever other identity markers might make us outsiders.

When Karyn Kusama says that Jennifer is "all id," she's describing a character who doesn't repress anything. One of the deepest pleasures of *Jennifer's Body* is indulging that odd, tantalizing impulse that wants to see her burn it all down and live to kill another day.

Conclusion: "I Am Still Socially Relevant"

"Can it even be considered a cult following at this point?" Megan Fox asked Diablo Cody of *Jennifer's Body* fandom in 2019. "I feel like it's broken through, where it's just a lot of people are obsessed with this movie."[1]

Despite Cody writing an Academy Award–winning film and Fox starring in some of the highest-grossing films of their release years, *Jennifer's Body* — the critically panned commercial failure — is the film that's remembered and celebrated most often for them both. "If somebody stops me," said Cody, "it's always some 22-year-old who wants to talk to me about *Jennifer's Body*, and to me that is the coolest thing in the world. Because it's like, I don't even think you could have legally seen this movie when it came out, and you found it."

The size of a film's following does impact how we categorize it, whether we call it "cult" or not, but that act of discovery that Cody describes points to a more satisfyingly cultish phenomenon. A lot of people are obsessed with *Jennifer's Body*, as Fox says, but there's a major difference between *Jennifer's Body* obsession and, say, the massive fandom surrounding Marvel's *Avengers* franchise. The latter is culturally inescapable, with the Disney-owned behemoth dominating comic book conventions and saturating the marketplace with advertisements, commercial product tie-ins, press junkets, and massive international rollouts on countless screens. Even if you don't seek Disney's output, it will find you. *Jennifer's Body* fans have to organize themselves, proselytize, write fan fiction, explain their obscure Halloween costumes, and — at least for a good decade before the film was "rescued" — protest that "actually, it's good!"

Sometimes cult films do break through. *Jennifer's Body* riffs on this reality when Colin invites Jennifer to see *The Rocky Horror Picture Show*, and she declines because she doesn't "like boxing movies." Jennifer is clearly fucking with him and is practiced in the art of rejecting boys. The joke lands precisely because *Rocky Horror* has become so ubiquitous even people in deepest Transylvania know it as the ultimate cult flick.

Reviews of *Jennifer's Body*'s sometimes did predict that its day might eventually come, or that at least its audience would someday find and cherish it. What a peculiar thing to not only recognize that taste is subjective and subject to all kinds of cultural and industrial forces, but also to recognize something in a film that *will* work with audiences someday . . . just not today. But that's what happened.

A.O. Scott defended *Jennifer's Body* in 2009 and wrote it "deserves — and is likely to win — a devoted cult following, despite its flaws."[2] Natasha Vargas-Cooper similarly declared, "*Jennifer's Body* aims to be a cult classic, and should be crowned as one."[3] Annalee Newitz was more skeptical about its chances in the cult pantheon, noting, "If the marketing droids at Fox had just been smart enough to realize that the movie was aimed at women — not unlike most horror movies — they might have had a cult hit on their hands."[4]

Some critics slammed *Jennifer's Body* for actively chasing cult status without bringing the necessary goods. Nick Pinkerton opined that, "A premeditated cult classic — they're kind of like 'pre-worn' designer jeans — *Jennifer's Body* seems designed more to be quoted than watched."[5] And Ben Child suggested its cult potential had already been written off: "reviewers seem to think the movie might even struggle to find a place on cult classic lists," he wrote, echoing the assumption that it was self-consciously aiming for cultdom.[6]

It didn't take too long for the cult to materialize, though. Or for its existence to be acknowledged. In a 2013 *BuzzFeed* appreciation listicle, Louis Peitzman claimed, "One day *Jennifer's Body* and Megan Fox will get the respect they deserve. Until then, Jennifer Check can enjoy her cult status."[7] Peitzman both predicted the eventual reckoning with the film's legacy and recognized its emerging cult following, just four years after its release. Three years after that, in 2016, Adam B. Vary, also in *BuzzFeed*, called the film a flop that became "a cult favorite" in his profile of Karyn Kusama,[8] while Nathalie Caron referred to it as "a cult movie" in her review of Kusama's *The Invitation* for *SyFy Wire*.[9]

The cult label fits *Jennifer's Body* in a few important ways, beyond its dedicated following. "A cult film can be seen as something that lacks the appeal of more mainstream fare, bringing to audiences an extra factor that can range from the challenging to the kitsch," writes Ian Haydn Smith, in his 2019 book *Cult Filmmakers*.[10] Ernest Mathijs and Jamie Sexton, in *Cult Cinema: An Introduction*, offer that "cult cinema is a kind of cinema identified by remarkably unusual audience receptions that stress the phenomenal component of the viewing experience, that upset traditional viewing strategies, that are situated at the margin of the mainstream, and that display reception tactics that have become a synonym for an attitude of minority resistance and niche celebration within mass culture."[11]

Both of these definitions stress how cult films oppose mainstream tastes and sensibilities. There's no single force in society called "the mainstream," but there do exist certain trends that hint at broad agreement on what's good, right, respectable, cool, and so on — at least at the moment. Megan Fox's much-derided tattoos were more mainstream in the 2000s than they would have been in earlier decades, for example, but since *Jennifer's Body* came out, they're so normal that being uninked is the rarity.

Before movements like #MeToo made it cool to care about systemic abuses, a film tackling industry sexism and abuse might be seen as preachy, and a film doing so through genre and subtext could be all but ignored. *Jennifer's Body* avoided the former label but occupied a different cultural space that could be dismissed as puerile trash.

The word "cult" itself hints at the heretical side of cult films, and how they thumb their noses at respectability or higher cultural tastes, whether that's because they're too progressive for the moment or just plain too offensive. A cult is seen as indoctrinating people into something less firmly established than traditional religions, less tested, less socially acceptable, and for those in the cult, that can be a badge of pride. Loving *Jennifer's Body* does mean ignoring its critical reception, its poor box-office showing, its various backlashes — or maybe loving it more *because* of its status as a castoff. It means embracing something without broader cultural support or approval. It means responding to the film, rather than an externally dictated taste hierarchy without objective merit.

Failure followed by intense celebration is an important part of the cult trajectory, and specifically so for *Jennifer's Body*, but there's more to cult films than opposition.

Jennifer's Body reflects a cultural moment, from Cody's use of slang, to the film's soundtrack, to teen style, to broader pop culture references (Dr. Phil, *Aquamarine*, Hannah Montana, and Zac Efron come to mind), to basic social dynamics of teenage life. Like its fellow cult films *Heathers* and *Jawbreaker* before it, it feels of its time not just in the way that all films are necessarily made at a specific point in history, but in the way that it immediately resonates on a deeper, barely tangible level.

Also like *Heathers* and *Jawbreaker*, it shifts tonally in dramatic ways, turning from innocent teen frivolity to murderous morbidity on a dime. Horror and comedy are in lockstep and create a cultish sense of hybridity, tonal ambiguity, transgression, and intertextuality, all common and important features of the cult experience, as laid out by Ernest Mathijs and Xavier Mendik in their introduction to *The Cult Film Reader*.[12]

The moral center of a lot of cult films is often as countercultural as its followings. By being mismarketed as a male gaze–centric, objectifying fantasy for teen boys, *Jennifer's Body* was primed to find a more discerning audience that could see through this framing and fall in love with the film on different terms. 20th Century Fox's misfire provided something to rally against, ultimately achieving its goal of hyping *Jennifer's Body*, if only by misreading the room so spectacularly as to delay the film's eventual success and cult reclamation. This reframing of the film by its audience comes with a cultish edge, or really two. On the one hand, it demands a rejection of the dominant narrative put out by 20th Century Fox (and plenty of critics), and on the other, it invites celebration of the genuinely queer and feminist themes at the core of *Jennifer's Body*, which are precisely what was missed, mocked, and misunderstood by a mainstream not sufficiently invested in either thing.

Attempts to reclaim or rehabilitate *Jennifer's Body* have come in waves over the years. "Let's get this out of the way first: *Jennifer's Body* is a criminally misunderstood modern-day horror classic," declared Louis Peitzman in 2013, adding that "Jennifer Check is an iconic horror movie villain . . . Or at least, she should be."[13] In 2015, Trace Thurman attempted to rescue *Jennifer's Body* from "*Juno* fatigue" and the film's detractors, offering the more tepid "I don't love it, but I've noticed myself liking it a little bit more every time I watch it."[14] Kalyn Corrigan called it "vastly under-appreciated" in 2016, while comparing its skillful exploration of toxic female friendship to that in the 2000 Canadian feminist werewolf classic *Ginger Snaps*,[15] and a year later Erin Sullivan wrote a piece for *Autostraddle* with the cheeky headline "I Watched Lesbianish Classic *Jennifer's Body* and Now I Love Cinema!!!"[16]

Just ahead of the film's tenth anniversary, the second wave suggested a consensus was beginning to form, bolstered by the #MeToo awakening. It felt more like a growing, interconnected movement. Critics, myself included, revisited the film in a variety of news and entertainment publications, looking specifically at the treatment of Megan Fox and the Diablo Cody backlash through a lens of systemic sexism. Terms like "ahead of its time," "relevant," and "necessary" weren't uncommon. In August 2018, Anne Cohen covered the mismarketing of the film and other injustices in a *Refinery29* series called "Writing Critics' Wrongs," in which "our female movie critic will give fresh consideration to the movies we love, hate, or love to hate" to adjust for the dominance of white male critics. "In a post-MeToo context," she said, "the idea of a woman's body being used for men's gain (even if it's a prize as lame as indie rock fame), and her coping with this violation by using her sexuality to entrap and feed on those who once objectified her, feels like something to be celebrated, not mocked."[17]

By the end of October 2018, there was enough of a shifting consensus for *Vox* to publish not just a reappraisal but a full-blown explainer of the "critical reevaluation of *Jennifer's Body*." In it, Constance Grady declared a "new consensus" that "2009 just wasn't ready for this movie." She added that *Jennifer's Body* has "become a case study in what we value in movies and what we dismiss, and how those values can shift over the course of a decade."[18]

Along with a few more think pieces, the second wave also featured some essential new interviews with Karyn Kusama, Diablo Cody, and Megan Fox, including Louis Peitzman's December 2018 Q&A in *BuzzFeed*, which revealed all kinds of new facts about the production and its mishandling by the marketing department, as well as everyone's feelings about the renewed interest from fans and critics. In it, Fox suggested that the film wasn't just mismarketed but also simply "ahead of its time," that society didn't seem ready for it in 2009, and that the film "may have been overshadowed by the unrelenting vampiric nature of the media's relationship to me at that time."[19] In a follow-up note on Twitter, Peitzman said, "I'm especially glad I was finally able to get Megan Fox to comment on *Jennifer's Body*, a movie I'd long feared she was ashamed of."

Now, *Jennifer's Body* seems to simply be accepted as canon, as a self-evident classic, worthy of best-of lists, like *Bloody Disgusting*'s 2020 "10 Best Coming-of-Age Horror Movies,"[20] or *Empire*'s "The 50 Greatest Teen Movies" from the same year.[21] Along with a slew of retrospectives came a sense of mainstream legitimacy. News stories about Fox, Cody, and Kusama feature *Jennifer's Body* more prominently since the film turned ten. Previously, a news item about Megan Fox being cast in *Teenage Mutant Ninja Turtles* or Diablo Cody producing a Broadway musical based on Alanis Morissette's *Jagged Little Pill* might not mention *Jennifer's Body* at all as part of either woman's portfolio. That's not the case anymore.

Throughout all of these phases, a lot of the spotlight has landed on Megan Fox specifically, highlighting the way the film industry used and objectified her, then turned its back on her when it was convenient. "We did Megan Fox wrong," the narrative goes; "We All Owe Megan Fox a Serious Apology, and Here Are the Receipts," reads one 2020 *BuzzFeed* headline.[22] There's a sense of justice being served every time a new starring role is announced for Fox, including, notably, new horror projects.

Still, Fox, Seyfried, Cody, and Kusama have all been busy since 2009. The need for a grand narrative tends to overwrite reality, and for all the talk of blacklisting and comebacks, they never went away. Cody and Fox most conspicuously shifted gears, Fox taking less high-profile roles and Cody moving away from her trademark quippy dialogue, albeit while continuing to write and direct prolifically. Fox has been steadily working, with new film and TV roles under her belt in any given year. Her career didn't manifest overnight thanks to Michael Bay, but he also didn't snuff it out. Seyfried, who managed to dodge most of the backlash and even won an MTV Movie Award for her work in *Jennifer's Body*, has had a consistent career with roles in commercially and critically successful projects. Kusama went from directing two studio films with A-list actors back-to-back to directing TV, before directing another feature-length film on a tiny indie budget six years later. But again, working on numerous award-winning series for prestige cable networks and streamers like AMC, Showtime, Amazon, and HBO isn't exactly slumming it or receding into obscurity. Her follow-up features *The Invitation* and *Destroyer* have been critically acclaimed and are frankly among the very best films of the 2010s.

Jennifer's Body was done dirty, no doubt, and the women at the center of it had to bear the brunt of various overlapping backlashes and antiquated industry rules, but their achievements speak for themselves and shouldn't be erased, lest we continue a toxic cycle of reducing women in Hollywood to their perceived failures.

Failure in Hollywood is a tenuous concept at best. The record is sometimes corrected; a film's legacy isn't forever cemented by bad box office earnings and a few hot takes in the moment. Famous films with famously meagre box office earnings include *Citizen Kane*, *It's a Wonderful Life*, *Vertigo*, *The Rocky Horror Picture Show*, *Blade Runner*, *Heathers*, *The Shawshank Redemption*, *Fight Club*, *Almost Famous*, *Donnie Darko*, *Wet Hot American Summer*, and *Mulholland Drive*. Most of these have gone on to become undisputed American classics, and others have huge cult followings.

Horror itself has gained more mainstream respectability in the intervening years, for one thing. The term "elevated horror" has been attached to films with heady subject matter or interesting aesthetics, including everything from *The Witch* to *Get Out* to *Hereditary*, and horror specifically dealing with gendered violence, sexual trauma, or victimization like *It Follows*, *Halloween*, *Black Christmas*, and *The Invisible Man* is talked about alongside broader cultural discussions of consent and rape culture, systemic sexism, and #MeToo. The 2019 documentary *Scream, Queen! My Nightmare on Elm Street* unpacked how queer subtext destroyed the legacy of *A Nightmare on Elm Street 2: Freddy's Revenge* — and the career of its gay star — but also how the film developed a fierce following within the queer community and has been reclaimed as a forgotten classic since its release in 1985.

Newer horror films aren't better than *Freddy's Revenge* or *Jennifer's Body*; we've just learned how to better evaluate a genre that used to be seen as trash, and how to empathize with the plight of characters not traditionally well represented, like a Black protagonist in *Get Out* or a queer former actor in *Scream, Queen!* "We" is a generalization, of course. Who determines when a genre has arrived and is worth cultural respect is hugely problematic, and that's why cult followings exist in the first place. The "we" of cult followings has always had the tools to look past mainstream dismissal and to empathize with outcasts. "Elevated horror" isn't a particularly neutral label to assign to a genre that has always dabbled in experimental practice, progressive politics, and important social commentary, but it's a sign that the broader culture is catching up, if slowly.

When Jennifer defiantly says, "I am still socially relevant," she could be talking about the film itself — just as defiant, if a little less doomed. She was always socially relevant, and she *is* still socially relevant. By straying from established and approved markers of taste, Diablo Cody and Karyn Kusama made something far more resonant than 2009 was ready for, and the resurrected *Jennifer's Body* is now having the last, well-deserved laugh.

*Endnotes

Introduction

1 Sonaiya Kelly, "How *Black Christmas* Became a 'Fiercely Feminist' Slasher Movie for the #MeToo Era," *Los Angeles Times*, December 11, 2019.

2 Clark Collis, "Jamie Lee Curtis Says the New *Halloween* is a #MeToo Movie," *Entertainment Weekly*, September 27, 2018.

3 Frederick Blichert, "*Jennifer's Body* Would Kill if It Came Out Today," *VICE*, October 23, 2018.

4 Constance Grady, "How *Jennifer's Body* Went from a Flop in 2009 to a Feminist Cult Classic Today," *Vox*, October 31, 2018.

Chapter 1

1 "*Jennifer's Body* Reunion: Megan Fox and Diablo Cody Get Candid about Hollywood (Exclusive)," *ET Live*, YouTube, September 19, 2019.

2 Emily VanDerWerff, "The Life, Death, and Rebirth of *Jennifer's Body*, According to Screenwriter Diablo Cody," *Vox*, November 28, 2018.

3 *Jennifer's Body* press conference, Toronto International Film Festival, September 11, 2009 (adambrodyvideos: YouTube, February 12, 2013).

4 *Jennifer's Body* press conference.

5 Jeff Baenen, "Ex-Stripper in Movie Spotlight," CNN, January 9, 2008.

6 "*Jennifer's Body* Reunion."

7 Mackenzie Nichols, "*Jennifer's Body* Turns 10: Megan Fox, Diablo Cody and Karyn Kusama Reflect on Making the Cult Classic," *Variety*, September 11, 2019.

8 "*Jennifer's Body* Reunion."

9 Adam B. Vary, "'I'm Not Going Away, People,'" *BuzzFeed*, April 7, 2016.

10 Adam B. Vary, "'I'm Not Going Away, People.'"

11 Adam B. Vary, "'I'm Not Going Away, People.'"

12 Anthony D'Alessandro, "How *Destroyer* Director Karyn Kusama Deconstructed the Noir Genre & Rebuilt It from a Woman's Point of View," *Deadline*, December 26, 2018.

13 Adam B. Vary, "'I'm Not Going Away, People.'"

14 Carol J. Clover, *Men, Women, and Chainsaws: Gender in the Modern Horror Film*, Princeton University Press, 2015, x.

15 Carol J. Clover, *Men, Women, and Chainsaws*, 39.

· Chapter 2

1 *Jennifer's Body* press conference.

2 Steven Zeitchik, "Fox Atomic Brings New Twists," *Variety*, February 18, 2007.

3 Nikki Finke, "Fox Atomic's Marketing Operations Fold," *Deadline*, January 11, 2008.

4 Gregg Kilday and Jay A. Fernandez, "Fox Shutting Down Atomic Label," *The Hollywood Reporter*, April 20, 2009.

5 Scott Tobias, "*Jennifer's Body*," *The A.V. Club*, September 17, 2009.

6 *Jennifer's Body* press conference.

7 Marshall Heyman, "Megan Fox," *Wonderland*, September 24, 2009.

8 Erin Carlson, "*Juno* Writer Feeling Hollywood Backlash," *Toronto Star*, February 27, 2008.

9 Peter Sciretta, "TIFF Review: *Jennifer's Body*," *Slashfilm*, September 10, 2009.

10 Louis Peitzman, "You Probably Owe *Jennifer's Body* an Apology," *BuzzFeed News*, December 7, 2018.

11 Emily VanDerWerff, "The Life, Death, and Rebirth of *Jennifer's Body*, According to Screenwriter Diablo Cody," *Vox*, November 28, 2018.

12 Bailey Calfee, "Why the Director of *Destroyer* and *Jennifer's Body* Makes Films about Strong Women," *Nylon*, January 17, 2019.

13 Anthony D'Alessandro, "How *Destroyer* Director Karyn Kusama Deconstructed the Noir Genre & Rebuilt It from a Woman's Point of View."

14 Roger Ebert, "Popular Girl Goes Bad, Begins to Devour Teen Flesh," RogerEbert.com, September 16, 2009.

15 Kirk Honeycutt, "*Twilight*: Film Review," *The Hollywood Reporter*, November 20, 2008.

16 Steve Newton, "*Twilight* Hunts Predictable Action-Thriller Territory," *The Georgia Straight*, November 21, 2008.

17 Sukhdev Sandhu, "*Twilight* — Review: First Love and Fresh Blood," *The Telegraph*, December 19, 2008.

18 Kira Cochrane, "*Jennifer's Body*: A Feminist Slasher Film? Really?" *The Guardian*, November 2, 2009.

19 Stephanie Zacharek, "The Naked Opportunism of *Jennifer's Body*," *Salon*, September 18, 2009.

20 Louis Peitzman, "You Probably Owe *Jennifer's Body* an Apology."

21 "*Jennifer's Body* Reunion."

22 Lena Wilson, "Diablo Cody Talks *Tully*, Feminist Filmmaking, and the Underrated *Jennifer's Body* [Interview]," *The Playlist*, May 1, 2018.

Chapter 3

1 Louis Peitzman, "You Probably Owe *Jennifer's Body* an Apology."

2 Marshall Heyman, "Megan Fox."

3 Jason Solomons, "Trailer Trash," *The Guardian*, July 5, 2009.

4 Roger Ebert, "Popular Girl Goes Bad, Begins to Devour Teen Flesh."

5 Lynn Hirschberg, "The Self-Manufacture of Megan Fox," *New York Times Magazine*, November 11, 2009.

6 *Jennifer's Body* press conference.

7 Hannah Ewens, "*Jennifer's Body* Captured Myspace-Emo Camp in All Its Glory," *VICE*, November 6, 2018.

8 Harry M. Benshoff, *Monsters in the Closet: Homosexuality and the Horror Film*, Manchester University Press, 1997, 2.

9 Mark Kirby, "Megan Fox Says What She Thinks and Does What She Wants," *GQ*, September 1, 2008.

10 David Katz, "Good Morning, Megan," *Esquire*, June 2009.

11 Jordan Crucchiola, "'It Was a Dark Time': Megan Fox and Karyn Kusama Revisit the *Jennifer's Body* Backlash," *Vulture*, October 1, 2019.

12 "The Year in Women 2008–2009: A Timeline," *Esquire*, October 5, 2009.

13 Mark Kirby, "Megan Fox Says What She Thinks and Does What She Wants."

14 Hannah Ewens, "*Jennifer's Body* Captured Myspace-Emo Camp in All Its Glory."

15 Amy Phillips, "The Seth Effect: The Revolution Is Coming, and It Listens to Death Cab for Cutie," *Willamette Week*, May 4, 2004.

Chapter 4

1 *Jennifer's Body* premiere post-screening Q&A, Toronto International Film Festival, September 11, 2009 (Robert Aaron Mitchell: YouTube, April 14, 2015).

2 "*Jennifer's Body* Reunion."

3 Andrew Unterberger, "The Story of Low Shoulder from *Jennifer's Body*, the Funniest and Most Disturbing Fictional Indie Rock Band Ever." *Billboard*, September 12, 2019.

4 Mark Kirby, "Megan Fox Says What She Thinks and Does What She Wants."

5 "*Jennifer's Body* Reunion."

6 Lena Wilson, "Diablo Cody Talks *Tully*, Feminist Filmmaking, and the Underrated *Jennifer's Body* [Interview]."

7 Genevieve Smith, "In Conversation: Diablo Cody: The Oscar-winning Screenwriter on the Fempire, her Megan Fox Therapy Breakthrough, and *Jagged Little Pill* the Musical." *Vulture*, November 19, 2019.

8 Marshall Heyman, "Megan Fox."

9 Nikki Finke, "Michael Bay's Crew Bitchslaps Megan Fox," *Deadline*, September 12, 2009.

10 Nikki Finke, "Michael Bay Speaks Up: 'I Don't Condone Crew Letter or Megan Fox's Quotes,'" *Deadline*, September 13, 2009.

11 Jordan Crucchiola, "'It Was a Dark Time.'"

12 Sean Fennessy, "Exclusive: The Break-Up of Michael Bay and Megan Fox," *GQ*, June 20, 2011.

13 Jeff Sneider, "Megan Fox Quit *Transformers* Over Michael Bay's Abuse." *TheWrap*, May 20, 2010.

14 Emily VanDerWerff, "The Life, Death, and Rebirth of *Jennifer's Body*, According to Screenwriter Diablo Cody."

15 Rebecca Rubin, "Ashley Judd, Mira Sorvino Respond to Peter Jackson's Claims that Weinstein Blacklisted Them," *Variety*, December 15, 2017.

16 "*Jennifer's Body* Reunion."

17 Louis Peitzman, "You Probably Owe *Jennifer's Body* an Apology."

18 Genevieve Smith, "In Conversation: Diablo Cody: The Oscar-winning Screenwriter on the Fempire, her Megan Fox Therapy Breakthrough, and *Jagged Little Pill* the Musical."

19 "*Jennifer's Body* Reunion."

20 Constance Grady, "How *Jennifer's Body* Went from a Flop in 2009 to a Feminist Cult Classic Today."

21 Alexandra Heller-Nicholas, *Rape-Revenge Films: A Critical Study*, McFarland & Company, 2011, 3.

22 Robin Wood, "Return of the Repressed," *Film Comment*, July/August 1978, 27.

23 Robin Wood, "Return of the Repressed," 26.

24 Ernest Mathijs and Jamie Sexton, *Cult Cinema: An Introduction*, Blackwell Publishing, 2012, 195.

25 Ernest Mathijs and Jamie Sexton, *Cult Cinema: An Introduction*, 198.

26 Jordan Crucchiola, "'It Was a Dark Time.'"

27 Barbara Creed, *The Monstrous-Feminine: Film, Feminism, Psychoanalysis*, Routledge, 2007, 3.

28 *Jennifer's Body* press conference.

Conclusion

1 "*Jennifer's Body* Reunion."

2 A.O. Scott, "Hell Is Other People, Especially the Popular Girl," *New York Times*, September 17, 2009.

3 Natasha Vargas-Cooper, "Review: Wicked, Smart *Jennifer's Body* Not Just About Megan Fox's Body," *E! Online*, September 17, 2009.

4 Annalee Newitz, "Did Stupid Marketing Kill *Jennifer's Body*?" *io9*, October 7, 2009.

5 Nick Pinkerton, "*Jennifer's Body* Eats Men, Forces Awkward Teen Dialogue," *Village Voice*, September 15, 2009.

6 Ben Child, "*Jennifer's Body* Gets a Critical Battering," *The Guardian*, September 17, 2009.

7 Louis Peitzman, "Why Megan Fox in *Jennifer's Body* Is One of the Greatest Horror Villains Ever," *BuzzFeed*, May 16, 2013.

8 Adam B. Vary, "'I'm Not Going Away, People.'"

9 Nathalie Caron, "This Tense New Trailer for Karyn Kusama's *The Invitation* Will Unnerve You," *SyFy Wire*, February 15, 2016.

10 Ian Haydn Smith, *Cult Filmmakers*, White Lion Publishing, 2019, 6.

11 Ernest Mathijs and Jamie Sexton, *Cult Cinema: An Introduction*, 8.

12 Ernest Mathijs and Xavier Mendik, "Editorial Introduction: What Is Cult Film?" *The Cult Film Reader*, Open University Press, 2008, 2–3.

13 Louis Peitzman, "Why Megan Fox in *Jennifer's Body* Is One of the Greatest Horror Villains Ever."

14 Trace Thurman, "In Defense of *Jennifer's Body*," *Bloody Disgusting*, February 27, 2015.

15 Kalyn Corrigan, "The Toxic Female Friendships in *Ginger Snaps* and *Jennifer's Body*," *Birth.Movies.Death.*, October 20, 2016.

16 Erin Sullivan, "I Watched Lesbianish Classic *Jennifer's Body* and Now I Love Cinema!!!" *Autostraddle*, October 27, 2017.

17 Anne Cohen, "*Jennifer's Body* & the Feminist Revenge Hero Who Came Too Early." Refinery29, August 3, 2018.

18 Constance Grady, "How *Jennifer's Body* Went from a Flop in 2009 to a Feminist Cult Classic Today."

19 Louis Peitzman, "You Probably Owe *Jennifer's Body* an Apology."

20 Meagan Navarro, "Growing Pains: The 10 Best Coming-of-Age Horror Movies," *Bloody Disgusting*, April 24, 2020.

21 Ben Travis, James White, Ian Freer, James Dyer, Alex Godfrey, Nick De Semlyen, Ella Kemp, Chris Hewitt, "The 50 Greatest Teen Movies," *Empire*, July 24, 2020.

22 Shelby Heinrich, "We All Owe Megan Fox a Serious Apology, and Here Are the Receipts," *BuzzFeed*, September 5, 2020.